Answers to Everyday Questions 3

<Intermediate>

身近な不思議を英語で学ぶ

＜中級＞

Arnold Arao
Kei Mihara
Yoshinori Miwa
Hiroshi Kimura

NAN'UN-DO

Answers to Everyday Questions 3
<Intermediate>

Arnold Arao
Kei Mihara
Yoshinori Miwa
Hiroshi Kimura

Download Audio
音声ファイル
無料 DL
のご案内

このテキストの音声を無料で視聴（ストリーミング）・ダウンロードできます。自習用音声としてご活用ください。
以下のサイトにアクセスしてテキスト番号で検索してください。

https://nanun-do.com　テキスト番号［**512146**］

※ 無線 LAN（WiFi）に接続してのご利用を推奨いたします。

※ 音声ダウンロードは Zip ファイルでの提供になります。
お使いの機器によっては別途ソフトウェア（アプリケーション）の導入が必要となります。

Read by
Anya Floris
Chris Koprowski

※ Answers to Everyday Questions 3 音声ダウンロードページは以下の QR コードからもご利用になれます。

はじめに

私たちの身の回りには不思議なことが溢れています。不思議な事象について、「なぜ？」と疑問を抱くことがあるでしょう。そこから不思議の扉が開き、思いがけない楽しい知識の冒険が始まるのです。ふと生じる「なぜ？」に耳を傾け、身近にある不思議な事象を楽しみながら考えてみましょう。

「なぜ？」と問う好奇心を持つことで、普段は気づかないことに気づくことができます。好奇心は、学びたいという欲求の源泉で、知りたいと思うことの原動力なのです。それは勉強の楽しさを育むワクワクする芽で、大事に育てたいものです。

本書では、私たちの日常の暮らしの中で不思議と思う、素朴な疑問を学びます。例えば「Tシャツ大流行のきっかけは？」「スニーカーの由来は？」などなど、身近にある不思議に目を向けて考えることは、知的好奇心を刺激し、さらに、様々な社会的・文化的事象に目を向けるきっかけになります。身近な不思議は意外とたくさんあります。そこで、学生にとって、できるだけ興味深く、おもしろい 15 のトピックを選びました。

本書は基本英文法を再確認し、知識や技能だけでなく、「考える」英語力を身に付けることを目的とした、中級レベルの英語総合教材です。「考える」英語力を養うため、主体性や思考力などを多面的に問う効果的に配置された練習問題を解くことで、リーディング、リスニング、ライティングの力を無理なく、バランスよく伸ばすことができます。

本書の特長

1. 単語の意味をチェックすることで、語彙力を増強
2. 240 語程度のエッセイを読むことで、リーディング力を強化
3. 60 語程度の会話を聴くことで、リスニング力をアップ
4. 80 語程度の空所補充問題をこなすことで、表現力を定着
5. 文法問題を解くことで、文法力を向上
6. 英文を書くことで、ライティング力を習得

本書を通じて「なぜ？」という好奇心を呼び起こしつつ、英語力の涵養に役立てば、筆者にとってこれに勝る喜びはありません。

2023 年 1 月
著者一同

本書の構成と使い方

Warm-up
質問に英語で答えます。

1 Vocabulary

各ユニットに出てくる単語を空所に入れて英文を完成します。

2 Reading

エッセイを読んで内容を理解します。

A True or False

英文が本文の内容に合っていれば T (True)、間違っていれば F (False) を選びます。

B Skimming and Scanning

本文の内容について、最も適切な答えを (A) ～ (C) から選びます。

3 Conversation

A Listen and Write

会話を聞いて空所に単語を書きます。

B Listen and Choose

質問を聞いて空所に単語を書き、最も適切な答えを (A) ～ (C) から選びます。

4 Text Completion

文章を完成するため、空所に入れる最も適切な語句や文を (A) ～ (C) から選びます。

5 Grammar

指示に従って文法問題を解きます。

6 Composition

A 日本語に合うように (　　) 内の語句を正しく並べ替えます。

B 質問に対する応答文を (　　) 内の語句を使って自由に書きます。

Grammar Spotlight
各ユニットの文法・語法を確認します。

Contents

Unit 1　What Did People Use Before Erasers? 7
消しゴムが発明される前に使っていたものは？
● 現在時制・過去時制

Unit 2　Who Is Barbie? 13
バービー人形の本当の名前は？
● 助動詞

Unit 3　How Did T-shirts Become Popular? 19
Tシャツ大流行のきっかけは？
● 完了形

Unit 4　Who Invented Cotton Candy? 25
綿菓子を発明したのは誰？
● 受動態

Unit 5　Which Came First, the TV or the RC? 31
テレビとリモコンの発明はどちらが先？
● There 構文

Unit 6　Why Do ATM PINs Have Only Four Numbers? 37
なぜ暗証番号は4桁の数字？
● 冠詞・名詞

Unit 7　Why Are Pencils Yellow? 43
なぜ鉛筆の始まりは黄色？
● 不定詞・動名詞

Unit 8　What Are the Ends of Shoelaces Called? 49
靴ひもの先に付いているプラスチックの名前は？
● 形容詞・副詞

Unit 9　Why Are Gym Shoes Called "Sneakers"? 55
スニーカーの由来は？
● 比較

Unit 10 **Why Do We Drink So Much Coffee?** 61
コーヒーを飲む理由は？
● 前置詞

Unit 11 **Which Came First, Lighters or Matches?** 67
ライターとマッチの発明はどちらが先？
● 接続詞

Unit 12 **Why Is Meat from Pigs Called "Pork"?** 73
なぜ豚の肉はポーク？
● 付加疑問文・修飾語句

Unit 13 **Can You Wang a "Welly"?** 79
ウェリントンブーツ投げはスポーツ？
● 関係代名詞・関係副詞

Unit 14 **Why Do We Shake Hands?** 85
握手をする理由は？
● 分詞・分詞構文

Unit 15 **What Did the First Webcam See?** 91
最初のウェブカメラが映したものは？
● 話法・仮定法

Unit 1

What Did People Use Before Erasers?

▶ present tense / past tense

なぜ消しゴムでこすると、鉛筆で紙に書いた字がきれいに消えるのでしょうか。それは消すというよりも、鉛筆の黒鉛をゴムに吸い付けることで取り除いているからです。消しゴムが生まれるまで、人々はどのようにして消していたのか考えてみましょう。

Warm-up

次の質問に英語で答えなさい。

1. Do you still use erasers to correct your mistakes? Why or why not?
2. When you make a mistake on a test, how does it make you feel?

1 Vocabulary

英文の（　　）に入れる最も適切な単語を語群より選び、(A) 〜 (J) で答えなさい。

(A) ancient	(B) correct	(C) discovery	(D) durable	(E) fall
(F) fix	(G) improve	(H) mistake	(I) moist	(J) rub

1. Oh no! Sally made a (　　) on the history test. She wrote 2001 but the right answer is 2011!
2. I really want to (　　) my English speaking ability; so, I'm taking a conversation class.
3. Something is wrong with our TV. Would you call the store and ask if they can (　　) it?
4. That is (　　)! You're right. The capital of Australia is Canberra.
5. The (　　) Greeks invented many things that we still use today.
6. After the rain last night, the leaves and grass are still a little (　　).
7. If you (　　) the magic lamp, a genie comes out and gives you three wishes.
8. This backpack is so (　　). I've been using it for nearly ten years.
9. The (　　) of penicillin by Alexander Fleming in 1928 has saved millions of lives around the world.
10. Make sure you hold this sandwich carefully, or it will (　　) apart.

2 Reading

02

Mistakes happen. No one likes to make mistakes. But making mistakes is an important part of learning. When you make a mistake, you can see what you did wrong and how you can improve. When you write your answers in ink, you can use erasable pens or corrective fluid to fix your mistakes. When you write in pencil, you can use erasers to correct your errors. Erasers have been around for a long time. What did people use before erasers were invented?

In 1770, a British engineer named Edward Nairne picked up a piece of rubber and used it to rub pencil markings off a sheet of paper. This "accident" gave us the first "eraser." Before then, people used different items to correct their writing mistakes. Some ancient people used sandstone or pumice, and other people used moist pieces of bread. Although Nairne's eraser was much better than what was used before, it still had some problems. The rubber erasers often fell apart and they smelled bad, too.

The modern eraser didn't arrive until 1839. That's when Charles Goodyear discovered a way to make rubber more durable. His invention was called vulcanization. It not only made erasers popular, but it also made rubber tires possible.

Notes **corrective fluid**「修正液」 **be around for a long time**「長い間存在する」 **Edward Nairne**「エドワード・ネアン」(1726-1806) **pick up**「手に取る」 **rub ... off**「～をこすり落とす」 **fall apart**「ボロボロになる」 **vulcanization**「加硫」

Reading Comprehension

A True or False

次の英文が本文の内容と一致する場合は T、一致しない場合は F を選びなさい。

1. We cannot learn from our mistakes. [**T F**]

2. Before erasers were invented, people used bread to correct writing mistakes. [**T F**]

3. The invention that made erasers possible is also used to make tires. [**T F**]

B Skimming and Scanning

本文の内容について、最も適切な答えや語句を (A) ～ (C) から選びなさい。

1. Who used the first eraser made of rubber?
(A) Billy Pumice (B) Charles Goodyear (C) Edward Nairne

2. One of the problems with the first rubber erasers was that they ______.
(A) smelled bad (B) were too hard (C) were too wet

3. What is the name of the invention that made rubber more durable?
(A) Modernization (B) Rubberization (C) Vulcanization

3 Conversation

A Listen and Write

03

次の会話を聞いて、(　　) に単語を書きなさい。

W: What is it that you are doing?

M: I'm doing a crossword [1](　　　　　　　). By the way, how do you spell "sandwich"?

W: S-A-N-D-W-I-C-H

M: I knew I had spelled it [2](　　　　　　　). I added an extra H after the W.

W: Do you need some whiteout to [3](　　　　　　　) your mistake?

M: No, thanks. I'm [4](　　　　　　　) an erasable pen.

B Listen and Choose

04

質問を聞いて、(　　) に単語を書き、最も適切な応答を (A) ～ (C) から選びなさい。

1. The man (　　　　　　) (　　　　　) write "sandwich." (　　　　　) (　　　　　) did he actually write?

(A) Sandwhich　　(B) Shandwich　　(C) Sandwichh

2. (　　　　　) (　　　　　　) the man (　　　　　) whiteout?

(A) Because he already has some corrective fluid.

(B) Because he is using a pencil with an eraser.

(C) Because he is using an erasable pen.

Notes　**by the way**「ところで」　**whiteout**「修正液」　**erasable pen**「消せるボールペン」

4 Text Completion

次の文章を読んで、空所に入れる最も適切なものを (A) ～ (C) から選びなさい。

Do you know how an eraser works? The lead of pencils __1__ made from graphite, clay, and water. When you write on paper with a pencil, small pieces of graphite __2__ to the paper. Erasers do not actually rub the marks off the paper. Erasers are very sticky. When you rub an eraser on the paper, the graphite sticks to the eraser. This is because the material that the eraser is made of __3__.

1. (A) are　　(B) is　　(C) were

2. (A) stick　　(B) sticks　　(C) stuck

3. (A) is made from paper

(B) is stickier than the paper

(C) is whiter than the paper

5 Grammar

A (　　) 内の適切な動詞を選び、英文を完成しなさい。

1. One in four children (are / is) addicted to his or her smartphone.
2. Our team (are / is) winning the game now.
3. The committee (has / have) decided to discuss the issue with the president.
4. Once a month, the students in the English class (go / goes) on a field trip to the public library.
5. Only 30% of American university students (graduate / graduates).
6. Every year, a pod of whales (swim / swims) along the coast.

B (　　) 内の最も適切な動詞を選び、英文を完成しなさい。

1. A pack of dogs (run / running / runs) on the beach every morning.
2. A group of carolers (sing / sings / sang) a Christmas carol last night.
3. The police department (has / have / had) its annual Christmas party yesterday.
4. Nearly 50% of the students (attend / attends / attended) the football game yesterday afternoon.
5. The plane does not arrive at 10 a.m. It (arrive / arrives / arrived) at 10 p.m.
6. The doctors at that hospital (work / works / worked) as volunteers during last month's emergency.
7. The baby stopped crying when his mom (pick / picks / picked) him up.
8. The next train (leave / leaves / left) this evening at 18:00.

C 語群から適切な動詞を選び、過去形にして英文を完成しなさい。

carry	clap	close	cook	cry

1. Mom ________________ a delicious dinner last night.
2. The novel was so sad. Pamela ________________ after reading it.
3. The audience ________________ loudly at the end of the rock concert.
4. Karen's husband ________________ a shopping basket for her at the supermarket.
5. The little girl ________________ her eyes and immediately fell asleep.

D 前半に続く後半を (a) ～ (d) から選び、英文を完成しなさい。

1. Moist bread was used to erase pencil marks _____.
2. The important thing is to erase mistakes _____.
3. There is a flock of geese flying over us. I wonder _____.
4. On the field, there are some boys _____.

(a) as soon as possible once you spot them
(b) before rubber erasers came into use
(c) who are playing with a soccer ball
(d) where they are headed

6 Writing

A 日本語に合うように、(　　) 内の語句を並べ替えなさい。

1. Making mistakes can be good (for / from / if / learn / them / us / we).
間違いをすることは、私たちがそれらから学ぶのであれば、私たちにとって良いことになります。

2. In 1770, an English engineer named Edward Nairne accidentally (a piece of / and / discovered / instead of / picked up / rubber / some bread) that rubber would rub out pencil marks.
1770 年にエドワード・ネアンという名のイギリスの技術者が、偶然パンの代わりに一片のゴムを手に取り、ゴムが鉛筆の跡を消せることを発見しました。

B 次の質問に、(　　) 内の語句を使って答えなさい。

1. Which do you prefer to use, traditional pencils or mechanical pencils? Why?
(like to use [prefer to use] / run out of lead / lead replacements)

2. Some teachers say that writing with a pen is better than writing with a pencil because it helps students build more self-confidence. Do you agree or disagree?
(write in ink / have more self-confidence)

Grammar Spotlight

▶現在時制

現在の動作や状態、一般的な事実などを表すとき、動詞の「現在形」を使います。

1. 現在の動作

We **play** soccer every weekend.
Robert often **travels** by air.
Liz always **goes** to school by bicycle.
・always, often, sometimes, usually など頻度の副詞をよく伴います。

2. 現在の状態

Bella **lives** in the suburbs of Los Angeles.
Clark **likes** to take photos of flowers as a hobby.

3. 一般的な事実、ことわざ

Water **boils** at 100 degrees Celsius.
There **is** no royal road to learning.

▶過去時制

過去の動作や状態、事実などを表すとき、動詞の「過去形」を使います。

1. 過去の動作

Robert **hiked** through the countryside yesterday.
It **rained** hard last night.

2. 過去の反復動作

When he was a student, Justin **went** to school by train.

3. 過去の状態

At that time, Jennifer **lived** in Spain.
I **felt** cold because of the wind.
He **was** very humble.

4. 過去の事実

Donald Trump **was** the 45th President of the United States.

Unit 2

Who Is Barbie?

▶ modal verbs

あなたは幼いころ何で遊びましたか。楽しい遊びは想像力を育て、将来の夢や可能性を伸長します。アメリカで生まれ、今も世代を超えて世界中の子どもたちに愛されている、着せ替え人形「バービー」の誕生秘話について考えてみましょう。

Warm-up

次の質問に英語で答えなさい。

1. What was your favorite toy as a child?
2. What is your hobby?

1 Vocabulary

英文の（　　）に入れる最も適切な単語を語群より選び、(A) ～ (J) で答えなさい。文頭に来る語も小文字にしています。

(A) astronaut	(B) doll	(C) enduring	(D) famous	(E) gender
(F) icon	(G) image	(H) notice	(I) separate	(J) unfortunately

1. Michael Jackson is an (　　) of pop music, because he had such a big influence on the music world.
2. *Emma* is an (　　) classic of literature. It will be read forever.
3. Did you (　　) Sam's new haircut? He looks really different.
4. Neil Armstrong's dream was to become an (　　). He always wanted to travel to the moon.
5. It is important to (　　) your work life from your private life.
6. Japan still does not have (　　) equality. There are many more men than women in management positions.
7. Some celebrities are (　　) in their own country, but no one knows them when they travel overseas.
8. That singer has an excellent (　　). His fans believe he loves his family and is very kind.
9. The little girl's favorite toy is a stuffed cloth (　　) named Annie.
10. (　　), we had to cancel the play because of the COVID-19 pandemic.

2 Reading

05

Barbie is an enduring social icon. She is the most famous doll in the world. Children have been playing with this small plastic doll for over 50 years. In the mid-1950s, a successful American businessperson named Ruth Handler noticed her daughter playing with dolls made of paper. This gave Ruth an idea. She wanted to create a "real" doll for her daughter. In 1959, she invented an 11-inch (28 centimeters) plastic woman. Ruth named the doll Barbie, after her daughter, Barbara. In fact, not many people know that Barbie's full name is Barbara Millicent Roberts.

Ruth wanted her invention to inspire little girls. When children played with Barbie, Ruth wanted them to believe they could be or do anything. That's why Barbie has had over 200 different jobs and careers. She has been a computer programmer, an astronaut, and even a rapper. Kids who play with Barbie can imagine becoming successful, too. They can make believe they are a singer, a doctor, or a homemaker with a husband and children. Over the years, many other dolls have joined the Barbie family. Barbie has brothers, sisters, and even a pet horse.

Unfortunately, not everyone likes Barbie. Some believe that she gives women a bad image. As a result, Barbie has changed over the years. Today, there are African-American Barbies, Asian Barbies, and even a "wheelchair" Barbie.

Notes **"real" doll**「リアルドール」リアルな造形の人形 **name ... after**「･･･ を～にちなんで名付ける」 **make believe**「～のふりをする」 **homemaker**「主婦」 **not everyone**「誰もが～というわけではない」（部分否定） **as a result**「結果として」

Reading Comprehension

A True or False

次の英文が本文の内容と一致する場合は T、一致しない場合は F を選びなさい。

1. Barbie is famous only in the U.S. **[T F]**

2. Barbie first appeared in the 1960s. **[T F]**

3. Barbie has even been an astronaut. **[T F]**

B Skimming and Scanning

本文の内容について、質問に対する最も適切な答えを (A) ～ (C) から選びなさい。

1. Who did Ruth Handler name Barbie after?

(A) Another doll (B) Her best friend (C) Her daughter

2. How tall is Barbie?

(A) 11 centimeters (B) 28 centimeters (C) 28 inches

3. How many jobs has Barbie had?
(A) Fewer than 200 (B) More than 200 (C) Over 300

3 Conversation

A Listen and Write

06

次の会話を聞いて、(　　) に単語を書きなさい。

W: I want to buy my little sister a birthday present. Do you have any [1](　　　　　　)?

M: How about a Barbie?

W: I think my sister is a [2](　　　　　　) too old to play with dolls.

M: How old is she?

W: She's [3](　　　　　　) 10.

M: That's not too old. My sister played with dolls [4](　　　　　　) she was in her mid-teens!

B Listen and Choose

07

質問を聞いて、(　　) に単語を書き、最も適切な応答を (A) ～ (C) から選びなさい。

1. What does the woman (　　　　　　) (　　　　　) (　　　　　)?
(A) A birthday present (B) A Christmas present (C) Something for herself

2. (　　　　　) (　　　　　) (　　　　　) the woman's sister right now?
(A) Nine years old (B) Ten years old (C) Fifteen years old

Notes **in one's mid-teens**「十代の半ばで」

4 Text Completion

次の文章を読んで、空所に入れる最も適切なものを (A) ～ (C) から選びなさい。

Some countries separate boys' toys from girls' toys. They hope that boys __1__ choose only toys made for boys, and girls will choose toys made for girls. If you go shopping in the U.S., you __2__ notice something strange — the toys for boys and the toys for girls are in the same place in the store. __3__, children can choose whatever toy they want to play with, even if the toy was originally made for the opposite gender.

1. (A) couldn't (B) ought (C) will

2. (A) can't (B) did (C) may

3. (A) By putting all the toys in one place
(B) By selling more toys made for boys than for girls
(C) By showing girls' toys and boys' toys in different places

5 Grammar

A (　　) 内の適切なものを選び、英文を完成しなさい。

1. You (should / would) eat fewer sweets if you want to lose weight.
2. I'm sorry. I'm busy on Saturday. I (can't / won't) help you.
3. Yeah! We (will / would) go camping this weekend!
4. I (can't / couldn't) find my wallet yesterday.
5. You (must / can) try hard if you want to pass the course.
6. (Can / Will) I call you later?
7. My parents look tired. They (should / shouldn't) go away somewhere and relax.
8. I (could / should) study hard for the exam. I really want to do well.

B (　　) 内の最も適切なものを選び、英文を完成しなさい。

1. Tina isn't feeling well. She (can / may not / will) go to the party tonight.
2. Peter injured his leg in a bicycle accident and (can / couldn't / ought to) walk very well.
3. The Italian restaurant is always full. The food (must / must not / won't) be very good.
4. If you look carefully, you (may / can't / will not) see the nests in the trees.
5. Please move your car. You (cannot / might not / will not) park here.

C 語群の動詞と have to / has to とを組み合わせて、英文を完成しなさい。

clean	get	pay	read	~~see~~	wake

e.g. I have to see the dentist.

1. Emily is going to bed early. She ____________________ up early tomorrow.
2. I can't see very well these days. I think I ____________________ glasses or contact lenses.
3. Brian is studying journalism. He ____________________ a lot of books.
4. I have a part-time job. I ____________________ my school tuition by myself.
5. Your room is really messy. You ____________________ it.

D (　　) に used to / would を入れて、英文を完成しなさい。

1. When I was younger, I (　　　　　　) live in an apartment with my parents.
2. My family (　　　　　　) often go to the beach on weekends.
3. Sally (　　　　　　) have long hair, but now she has short hair.
4. Ms. Simmons (　　　　　　) be a teacher for many years.
5. When he was in university, Robert (　　　　　　) always study until late at night.

E 前半に続く後半を (a) ～ (d) から選び、英文を完成しなさい。

1. I will be out of town on business, _____.
2. After it stops raining, _____.
3. When Osamu was in high school, _____.
4. Justin spoke in a very loud voice _____.

(a) he could not speak English so well
(b) so I could understand what he said
(c) so I will not be able to attend the party
(d) we might be able to go to the beach

6 Writing

A 日本語に合うように、(　　) 内の語句を並べ替えなさい。

1. Ruth Handler (doll / for / got / the Barbie / the inspiration / watching / while) her young daughter, Barbara, play with dolls made of paper.
ルース・ハンドラーは、紙で作った人形で幼い娘のバーバラが遊ぶのを見ている間に、バービー人形の着想を得ました。

2. Little girls have always (able / and / been / different / play / roles / to) careers while playing with Barbie.
幼い女の子たちはバービーと遊びながら、いつも様々な役と職業を演じることができました。

B 次の質問に、(　　) 内の語句を使って答えなさい。

1. Do you think children should be allowed to play with any toy they want? Why or why not?
(play with any toy / an important part of)

2. Do you think that there are jobs that only men (or only women) can do better? Why?
(there are some jobs / one gender than another / physical strength)

Grammar Spotlight

▶助動詞

「助動詞＋動詞の原形」の形で使い、動詞に意味を加えます。

1. **will**：～だろう（未来）、～するつもりだ（意志）　＜過去形は **would**＞
   can：～できる（可能）、～してもよい（許可）　＜過去形は **could**＞
   may：～してもよい（許可）、～かもしれない（推量）　＜過去形は **might**＞
   should：～すべきだ（義務）、～するはずだ（推量）
   must：～しなければならない（義務）、～に違いない（推量）

   You **can** enjoy seeing tonight's concert online.
   I **must** buy a stuffed animal for my daughter.
   You **should** fill out the form carefully.
   Emily **will have to** go to the beauty salon.
   Eric **will be able to** leave the hospital soon.
   We **ought to** invite Amy to our party.

2. **過去の習慣 used to, would「以前は～だった、かつて～した」**

   ▶ 過去と現在との対比
   used to は、以前はしていたが、今はしていない習慣を表す。

   ▶ 過去の回想
   would は、過去にしていたことを表し、今のことについては明白ではない。
   always, often, when などと共に使うことが多い。

   There **used to** be a hotel here.
   「以前はここにホテルがありました」（今はもうない）
   Back then, I **would often** play the flute.
   「あのときは、よくフルートを吹いたものでした」（今も吹くかもしれない）

   ・状態を表す動詞には would は使いません。

   × He **would** live in Los Angeles.
   ○ He **used to** live in Los Angeles.

Unit 3
How Did T-shirts Become Popular?

▶perfect forms

誰もが当たり前に着ているＴシャツは、最もカジュアルなファッションアイテムと言えます。なぜＴシャツが世界中の人々に愛され、普段着としての地位を確立したのでしょうか。Ｔシャツの起源や、時代の流れの中でこれほどまで広まった理由を考えてみましょう。

Warm-up

次の質問に英語で答えなさい。

1. How often do you wear T-shirts? When do you wear them?

2. Do you like to wear unique kinds of clothing? Why or why not?

1 Vocabulary

英文の（　　）に入れる最も適切な単語を語群より選び、(A) ～ (J) で答えなさい。文頭に来る語も小文字にしています。

(A) combine	(B) comfortable	(C) common	(D) expression	(E) fabric
(F) fashionable	(G) lifestyle	(H) personality	(I) technology	(J) wardrobe

1. Musicians have a large (　　). They like to change their clothes often during a concert.

2. Often, clothes that are (　　) this year are out of style next year.

3. I really like these shoes. They are so (　　) and easy to walk in.

4. Sandra has a shy (　　). It is difficult for her to talk to people she does not know.

5. Alexa has a very active (　　). She plays sports, goes to lots of social events, and works part-time.

6. Wearable products like smart watches are very (　　) these days. Almost everyone has one.

7. Samuel gave flowers to his mother on Mother's Day as an (　　) of his thanks.

8. What color do you get when you (　　) red and yellow?

9. (　　) is developing so quickly. Every year, computers are getting faster and faster.

10. Donna was looking for a pretty (　　) to make a dress for her senior prom.

2 Reading 08

Today, T-shirts are an important part of everyone's wardrobe. They are cheap, fashionable, comfortable, and easy to wash and dry. They are made from many different materials and come in all kinds of colors and designs. People like to wear T-shirts with writing or pictures on them to express their personality and lifestyle. So, how did T-shirts become so popular?

Originally, T-shirts were worn under outer clothes as a kind of underwear. Sailors, for example, wore T-shirts called "union shirts" under their uniforms. Soon, other people started wearing "union shirts," but as an outer garment. They became known as T-shirts because of their T shape. In 1951, a T-shirt appeared in a movie for the first time. In the film *A Streetcar Named Desire*, an actor named Marlon Brando wore only a white T-shirt with a pair of jeans. Soon, this style became all the rage. Young men all across America—and in many parts of the world—began wearing T-shirts in the same way. It was a way for young people to express their freedom and individuality. T-shirts were suddenly "cool."

In the 1960s, T-shirts decorated with logos and images began to appear. Some of these designs, such as I♥NY, Hard Rock Cafe, Mickey Mouse, and Bob Marley, can still be seen everywhere.

Notes **outer garment**「上着」 **for the first time**「初めて」 ***A Streetcar Named Desire***『欲望という名の電車』アメリカ映画 **all the rage**「大流行」 **I♥NY**「アイ・ラブ・ニューヨーク」**love** を ♥ で表現

Reading Comprehension

A True or False

次の英文が本文の内容と一致する場合は T、一致しない場合は F を選びなさい。

1. People like to express their personality using T-shirts. [T F]
2. Originally, T-shirts were worn mainly by factory workers. [T F]
3. Wearing only T-shirts as an outer garment became popular because of a movie. [T F]

B Skimming and Scanning

本文の内容について、最も適切な答えを (A) ～ (C) から選びなさい。

1. What were T-shirts originally used for?
   (A) As a uniform (B) As advertising (C) As underwear
2. What was the name of the actor in *A Streetcar Named Desire*?
   (A) Bob Marley (B) Marlon Brando (C) Mickey Mouse
3. When did T-shirt logos start to become popular?
   (A) In the early 1950s (B) In the late 1950s (C) In the 1960s

3 Conversation

A Listen and Write

09

次の会話を聞いて、(　　) に単語を書きなさい。

M: Have you [1](   ) my Yankees T-shirt?
W: Did you [2](   ) the chest of drawers by the bed?
M: Yes, but it's not [3](   ).
W: Maybe it is in the laundry hamper.
M: Yes! Here it is!
W: You aren't going to [4](   ) it like that, are you?

B Listen and Choose

10

質問を聞いて、(　　) に単語を書き、最も適切な応答を (A) ～ (C) から選びなさい。

1. What is the man (   ) (   )?
(A) His baseball cap　　(B) His baseball T-shirt　　(C) His work shirt

2. (   ) (   ) the man's T-shirt?
(A) Under the bed　　(B) In the drawer　　(C) In the laundry hamper

---

Notes　**chest of drawers**「たんす」　**laundry hamper**「洗濯かご」　**here it is**「あったよ」

4 Text Completion

次の文章を読んで、空所に入れる最も適切なものを (A) ～ (C) から選びなさい。

"[*Some color*] is the new black." is a common fashion expression. Every year, clothing companies try to come up with the __1__ item of clothing. They __2__ colors and interesting designs with new materials. Their goal is to be this year's "new black." Now, a new technology might change that. Scientists in Canada have created a fabric that uses the electricity in the human body __3__ of a clothing's material. Can this fabric be the "new black"?

1. (A) popular　　(B) more popular　　(C) most popular
2. (A) combine　　(B) combined　　(C) will combine
3. (A) as changed the color
(B) as changing the color
(C) to change the color

Notes　**new black**「流行り」　**come up with**「～を考え出す」

5 Grammar

A (　　) 内の適切な語句を選び、英文を完成しなさい。

1. My grandmother (visits / has visited) many countries over the last ten years.
2. I (seen / have seen) that movie twice.
3. (Have you did / Have you done) your homework?
4. Oh, no! Irene (has broken / have broken) another glass.
5. It (has never snowed / never have snowed) like this before!

B (　　) 内の最も適切な語句を選び、英文を完成しなさい。

1. I (see / sees / have seen) that man before, but I can't remember where.
2. I (don't have / had not / haven't had) any problems so far.
3. We (play / played / have played) soccer yesterday afternoon.
4. James lives in Los Angeles. He (lives / lived / has lived) there all his life.
5. I went straight to bed when I (get / got / have got) home last night.

C 語群から適切な単語を選び、現在完了形にして英文を完成しなさい。

(finish / just)	(grow)	~~(read /already)~~	(ride)	(meet / not)	(pay / already)

e.g. I have already read the letter that Julie wrote.

1. Anna ____________________ the bullet train from Tokyo to Osaka once.
2. We ____________________ the famous author yet. We are still waiting.
3. My dad ____________________ for tonight's dinner. He got a bonus last week.
4. Henry ____________________ so much in one year! Look how tall he is!
5. They ____________________ painting the wall, so be careful.

D 前半に続く後半を (a) ～ (d) から選び、英文を完成しなさい。

1. Kenneth has already finished _____.
2. Monica has never been _____.
3. T-shirts have become _____.
4. I have not _____.

(a) overseas by herself
(b) had time to review the report
(c) doing his homework
(d) a means of self-expression

6 Writing

A 日本語に合うように、(　　) 内の語句を並べ替えなさい。

1. A T-shirt is a style of (after / and / its body / named / of / shirt / the T shape) sleeves.

T シャツは、胴体と袖の T 字型にちなんで名付けられたタイプのシャツです。

2. T-shirts became more (Marlon Brando / one / popular / the public / when / with / wore) in the movie *A Streetcar Named Desire.*

T シャツはマーロン・ブランドが映画『欲望という名の電車』で着たとき、一般の人々にさらに人気が出ました。

B 次の質問に、(　　) 内の語句を使って答えなさい。

1. What kind of fashion do you usually wear? Why?

(like to wear / because it is / easy to move)

2. Some people feel uncomfortable when they see men wearing women's clothing or women wearing men's clothing. What do you think about that?

(understand their feeling / a little shocked / different fashion styles)

Grammar Spotlight

▶完了形

1. 現在完了形：現在までの完了・経験・継続 < have / has +過去分詞 >

過去の動作や状態が今につながっているときに使用します。

Megan **has** just **got** to the venue.　（完了）
I **have been** to Ireland before.　（経験）
It **has been** sunny for a week.　（継続）

現在完了形とよく共に使う語：

- 完了：already, just, yet
- 経験：before, ever, once, never
- 継続：for, since

現在完了形は、現在とつながりのない過去を表す副詞 (ago, just now, last week [month, year], yesterday) や when と共には使用できません。

- × I **have been** to Hawaii twice when I was a student.
- ○ I **went** to Hawaii twice when I was a student.

2. 過去完了形 < had +過去分詞 >

過去のある時点までの完了・経験・継続を表すときに使用します。

When Frank arrived at the station, the train **had** already **left**.

3. 未来完了形 < will have +過去分詞 >

未来のある時点における完了・経験・継続を表すときに使用します。

Eric **will have finished** the assignment by Monday.

Unit 4

Who Invented Cotton Candy?

▶passive forms

お祭りやイベントに欠かせないものの１つが綿菓子です。子どものころワクワクしながら食べた思い出がある人もいるでしょう。ふわふわして甘い、白やピンクの綿菓子は、実はアメリカ発祥のお菓子です。綿菓子は誰が発明したのでしょうか。

Warm-up

次の質問に英語で答えなさい。

1. Do you like going to festivals?
2. What are some of the most popular or famous festivals in your hometown?

1 Vocabulary

英文の（　　）に入れる最も適切な単語を語群より選び、(A) 〜 (J) で答えなさい。

(A) eventually	(B) fluffy	(C) mouthwatering	(D) product	(E) snack
(F) souvenir	(G) spicy	(H) traditional	(I) treat	(J) vending

1. If I study English very hard and watch videos on YouTube and Netflix, (　　), I'm sure I'll become a good English speaker.
2. We should try that new Indian restaurant that opened on Broadway. Harry said their curry was a bit (　　) but very tasty.
3. My aunt brought me a nice (　　) from Okinawa. They're cookies made from purple sweet potatoes.
4. How cute those kittens are! They're all so small and (　　), like little clouds.
5. Hot dogs are a (　　) food that fans love to eat at baseball games in the U.S.
6. Today's (　　) machines are amazing. Some sell neckties, make-up, and even fresh-baked pizza.
7. I'm a little hungry. Do you have a little (　　) like some chips or crackers I could munch on?
8. A: Hey, Sally, can you give me another word for "delicious"?
   B: How about "(　　)"?
9. When you visit Seattle, don't forget to bring me back a (　　) like some postcards or a keychain.
10. Our company's latest (　　) is a sugar-free hot chocolate that tastes even better than the real thing.

2 Reading

In the U.K., it is called “candy floss”; in Australia, it is known as “fairy floss”; in Italy, people call it “sugar thread” or *zucchero filato*; in France, it is called “Papa’s Beard” or *la barbe a Papa*. This delicious treat was created in the late 19th century. Since then, it has not changed very much. Do you know what this sweet treat is?

In 1904, John C. Wharton and William J. Morrison debuted a new kind of candy machine at the St. Louis World’s Fair. Wharton, a dentist, and Morrison, a candy-maker, called their candy “fairy floss” because it was pink and fluffy. Their new product was a huge success! It became a popular treat at festivals, carnivals, and circuses all around the world. Eventually, Wharton and Morrison’s candy invention came to be known as “cotton candy.”

Over the years, the machines that make cotton candy have become bigger and better. There is even a new cotton candy vending machine that makes cotton candy right in front of you. Nowadays, you can try cotton candy in many different colors and flavors like mint, apple cider, and even bubble gum. Cotton candy is sweet and fun to eat. But what is the best thing about eating cotton candy? It has less sugar than a can of soda!

Notes **cotton candy**「綿菓子」 **sweet treat**「甘いもの、お菓子」 **St. Louis World’s Fair**「セントルイス万国博覧会」 **be known as**「〜として知られる」 **bubble gum**「風船ガム」

Reading Comprehension

A True or False

次の英文が本文の内容と一致する場合は T、一致しない場合は F を選びなさい。

1. In Italy, cotton candy is known as *la barbe a Papa*. [**T F**]

2. Cotton candy is a popular treat all over the world. [**T F**]

3. Cotton candy machine has not changed a lot since it first appeared. [**T F**]

B Skimming and Scanning

本文の内容について、空所に入れる最も適切な語句を (A) 〜 (C) から選びなさい。

1. Cotton candy debuted in St. Louis in _____ at a World’s Fair.
(A) 1809 (B) 1900 (C) 1904

2. The original name of cotton candy given to it by its inventors was _____.
(A) candy floss (B) fairy floss (C) Papa’s Beard

3. Cotton candy has _____ a can of soda.
(A) less sugar than (B) more sugar than (C) the same amount of sugar as

3 Conversation

A Listen and Write

12

次の会話を聞いて、（　　）に単語を書きなさい。

W: Let's check out the food vendors and get something to eat.
M: Sure. What do you have in [1](　　　　　　)?
W: I haven't [2](　　　　　　　　) a corn dog in a while. I could really go for one.
M: Oh, that sounds yummy!
W: How about you? Is there anything [3](　　　　　　　　　) you would like to eat?
M: Well, that taffy apple [4](　　　　　　　　) mouthwatering.

B Listen and Choose

13

質問を聞いて、（　　）に単語を書き、最も適切な応答を (A) ～ (C) から選びなさい。

1. (　　　　　　) is the woman (　　　　　　　　　　)(　　　　　) getting?
(A) A corn dog　(B) Cotton candy　(C) A taffy apple

2. (　　　　　　) is the man (　　　　　　　　　　)(　　　　　)?
(A) A corn dog　(B) Cotton candy　(C) A taffy apple

Notes **food vendor**「フードベンダー」食べ物を売る屋台　**corn dog**「アメリカンドッグ」　**in a while**「しばらくの間」　**could really go for**「～が本当に食べたいな」　**taffy apple**「リンゴ飴」　**mouthwatering**「美味しそうな」

4 Text Completion

次の図表を見て、質問に対する最も適切なものを (A) ～ (C) から選びなさい。

	Calories	Fat	Sodium	Sugar	Cholesterol
Cotton candy	105	0.0 g	0.0 mg	26.0 g	0.0 mg
Caramel popcorn	230	4.0 g	150 mg	25.0 g	0.0 mg
Corn dog	350	20.0 g	1000 mg	11.0 g	37 mg
Soda	180	0.0 g	0.0 mg	10.6 g	0.0 mg
Grilled chicken	177	16.0g	600 mg	2.9 g	120 mg
Grilled squid	290	3.0 g	690 mg	12.24 g	608 mg

1. Which snack has the most calories?
(A) Corn dog　(B) Cotton candy　(C) Grilled squid

2. Which snack has the least fat?
(A) Caramel popcorn　(B) Cotton candy　(C) Grilled squid

3. Which snack has the most sodium?
(A) Caramel popcorn　(B) Corn dog　(C) Grilled chicken

4. Which snack has the least sugar?
(A) Corn dog　(B) Grilled chicken　(C) Soda

5. Which snack has the most cholesterol?
(A) Corn dog　(B) Grilled chicken　(C) Grilled squid

5 Grammar

A (　　) 内の適切な語句を選び、受動態の英文を完成しなさい。

1. Many people read the novel last year.
→ The novel (is read / was read) by many people last year.

2. Everybody loves chocolate cake!
→ Chocolate cake (is loved / was loved) by everybody!

3. The manager receives many emails every day.
→ Many emails (is received / are received) by the manager every day.

4. Ms. Sanderson teaches Business English.
→ Business English (are taught / is taught) by Ms. Sanderson.

5. The company pays their employees on Friday.
→ The employees (are paid / is paid) by the company on Friday.

B (　　) 内の最も適切な語句を選び、英文を完成しなさい。

1. The flowers (water / is watered / are watered) by her every day.
2. Every morning the door (opens / was opened / is opened) for me by the janitor.
3. The office (cleans / cleaned / is cleaned) every afternoon.
4. This castle (built / is built / was built) 400 years ago.
5. *Romeo and Juliet* (wrote / are written / was written) by Shakespeare.
6. The first James Bond movie (releases / released / was released) in 1962.
7. No food or drink (allow / is allowed / are allowed) in the computer lab.

C 語群から動詞を選び、適切な形にして能動態と受動態の英文を完成しなさい。

buy	eat	see	speak	take

1. a. Sally (　　　　　　　　) your pizza last night.
b. Your pizza (　　　　　　　　) by Sally last night.

2. a. Daniel (　　　　　　　　) Stephen King's new book last week.
b. Stephen King's new book (　　　　　　　　) by Daniel last week.

3. a. A stranger (　　　　　　　　) to me on the train yesterday.
b. I (　　　　　　　　) to on the train by a stranger yesterday.

4. a. We can (　　　　　　　　) many stars here tonight because the sky is clear.
b. Many stars can (　　　　　　　　) here tonight because the sky is clear.

5. a. My mother (　　　　　　　　) me to school every morning.
b. I am (　　　　　　　　) to school by my mother every morning.

D 前半に続く後半を (a) ～ (d) から選び、英文を完成しなさい。

1. Cotton candy is fun to watch as it is _____.
2. An announcement was made to _____.
3. The schedule was decided _____.
4. The woman was taken to the hospital _____.

(a) after the accident
(b) by the manager last week
(c) spun in a special machine
(d) the students on Friday afternoon

6 Writing

A 日本語に合うように、(　　) 内の語句を並べ替えなさい。

1. Cotton candy was invented by a dentist and a candy-maker. It was introduced at the 1904 World's Fair (an international / and / been / ever / has / hit / since).
綿菓子は、歯医者とキャンディー製造業者によって発明されました。1904年の万国博覧会で出品され、それ以来国際的なヒットになっています。

2. Cotton candy is a light (and / candy / cotton wool / fluffy / resembles / sugar / that). You can find it at every fair and amusement park.
綿菓子は、原綿に似ている軽くてふわふわした砂糖菓子です。あらゆるお祭りや遊園地で見ることができます。

B 次の質問に、(　　) 内の語句を使って答えなさい。

1. When you go to festivals or amusement parks, what foods do you like to eat?
(I like to / grilled chicken / corn dogs)

2. Some people say that young Japanese eat too much junk food. Do you agree or disagree?
(a lot of junk food / fast food restaurants / McDonald's)

Grammar Spotlight

▶受動態

受動態は、主語が動作を受ける対象になる文で、「(主語が) ～される」という形で使われます。

1. 受動態：be 動詞＋過去分詞＋ (by ～)

The laundry **is done** by Mom every day.
News reports **are written** by reporters.
The room **was cleaned** well by Anna.

2. 能動態と受動態の書き換え

未来形の受動態 ＜will be + 過去分詞＞

I **will meet** my friend at the airport.
→ My friend **will be met** by me at the airport.

進行形の受動態 ＜be being + 過去分詞＞

Lily **is baking** some brownies.
→ Some brownies **are being baked** by Lily.

完了形の受動態 ＜have / has been + 過去分詞＞

I **have cooked** dinner.
→ Dinner **has been cooked** by me.

3. by 以外の前置詞

The pop singer **is known to** everyone.
The city hall **is built of** brick.
The town **was covered with** snow.

Unit 5
Which Came First, the TV or the RC?

▶ there-constructions

人は常に便利さを求めます。私たちの生活の中に登場したテレビと、操作アイテムとしてのリモコンは、それぞれ発明以来進化しています。現代のテクノロジーのシンボルといえるテレビとリモコンは、どちらが先に発明されたのでしょうか。

Warm-up

次の質問に英語で答えなさい。

1. What kind of TV programs do you like to watch?
2. How much time do you spend each day watching TV?

1 Vocabulary

英文の（　　）に入れる最も適切な単語を語群より選び、(A) ～ (J) で答えなさい。

(A) cable	(B) channel	(C) commercial	(D) debut	(E) inventor
(F) manufacturer	(G) object	(H) puppet	(I) remote	(J) sensitive

1. Oh! It's time for the Giants-Tigers game to start. Could you please change the (　　) for me?
2. It's too cold in here. Where is the (　　) for the air conditioner?
3. Tim Berners-Lee is the (　　) of the world wide web, which he created in 1989.
4. The first radio made its (　　) in 1894. It was invented by Guglielmo Marconi.
5. One student made a cute hand (　　) from an old sock, buttons, and some pieces of cloth.
6. While he was out camping, George looked up and saw a strange, green (　　) flying across the sky.
7. First, connect the (　　) from your printer to the back of your PC.
8. This microphone is very (　　). It can pick up small noises from very far away.
9. Our company makes toys. In fact, we are the largest (　　) of toy robots in the world.
10. There is a funny TV (　　) that shows a father using his GPS to follow his daughter on a date.

2 Reading 14

Today, we use remote controls for all kinds of things: turning lights on and off, playing music, opening and closing garage doors—even controlling pet dogs. But the remote control we use most often turns our TV on and off, changes channels, and controls the volume. But do you know which came first, the TV or the TV remote control?

The first real television made its debut in October 1925. That's when Scottish inventor John Logie Baird showed an image of a ventriloquist's puppet named Stooky Bill. The next year, Japanese inventor Kenjiro Takayanagi introduced a simple television system at Hamamatsu Technical High School. And in 1927, an American named Philo Farnsworth demonstrated his own unique TV system.

But what about the remote control? Actually, the first remote control came nearly 30 years before the invention of the TV. It was created in 1898 by the Serbian inventor Nikola Tesla, who wanted to control objects from far away. He came up with the idea for what he called "teleautomation." He first used his invention to remote control a small boat.

It wasn't until 1956 that the first modern TV remote control appeared. The president of Zenith, a TV manufacturer, didn't like watching TV commercials. One of his company's engineers, Robert Adler, designed a remote control that could change the channels. This meant that his "boss" didn't have to sit through commercials, and he didn't have to get up off his sofa to change channels, either.

Notes **turn ... on and off**「～をつけたり消したりする」 **ventriloquist's puppet**「腹話術師の人形」 **Philo Farnsworth**「フィロ・ファーンズワース」アメリカの発明家 **Serbian**「セルビア人の」 **from far away**「遠くから」 **come up with**「思いつく」

Reading Comprehension

A True or False

次の英文が本文の内容と一致する場合は T、一致しない場合は F を選びなさい。

1. Remote controls have many different uses. [**T F**]

2. The first television was demonstrated in autumn 1925. [**T F**]

3. The modern remote control was first appeared in 1898. [**T F**]

B Skimming and Scanning

本文の内容について、最も適切な答えや語句を (A) ～ (C) から選びなさい。

1. According to the author, the first person to show a television image was from _____.
(A) America (B) Scotland (C) Serbia

2. Nicola Tesla demonstrated his "teleautomaton" by controlling a small _____.
(A) car (B) boat (C) puppet

3. The modern remote was invented because one company president did not like _____.
(A) changing channels (B) sitting on his sofa (C) TV commercials

3 Conversation

A Listen and Write

15

次の会話を聞いて、(　　) に単語を書きなさい。

W: What's on TV? Anything interesting?
M: Let's see. What do you feel like watching?
W: Anything 1(　　　　　) a horror film is okay with me.
M: Really? There's a 2(　　　　　　　) horror film streaming on Netflix right now.
W: No, thank you. I can never 3(　　　　　　) after watching a horror film.
M: Okay. Well, how 4(　　　　　　) a whodunit?
W: Sounds good. I enjoy a good mystery.

B Listen and Choose

16

質問を聞いて、(　　) に単語を書き、最も適切な応答を (A) ～ (C) から選びなさい。

1. What (　　　　　) the woman NOT (　　　　　　　) (　　　　) (　　　　　　　)?
(A) A horror movie (B) A mystery (C) Anything on TV

2. What (　　　　　) the man and woman (　　　　　　　　) (　　　　　　)?
(A) A horror movie (B) A mystery (C) Nothing at all

Notes **let's see**「ええと」 **feel like -ing**「～したい気がする」 **stream**「ストリーム配信する」 **Netflix**「ネットフリックス」動画配信サービス

4 Text Completion

次の文章を読んで、空所に入れる最も適切なものを (A) ～ (C) から選びなさい。

Remote controls are convenient. Just press the button on your TV's remote, __1__ you can change channels and control the volume without moving. The first remote controls were different from today's, however. There __2__ a short cable connected to the television and the remote could only turn the TV on and off. Later, a "cable-less" remote control was invented that could also change channels. This newer remote used light, but unfortunately, these light-based remote controls were a little too sensitive to light. __3__

1. (A) and (B) but (C) or

2. (A) are (B) was (C) were

3. (A) Many people would watch TV at the same time.
(B) On a sunny day, the channel would sometimes change automatically.
(C) We would often watch TV while eating dinner.

5 Grammar

A (　　) 内の適切な単語を選び、英文を完成しなさい。

1. There (is / are) very useful information to be found on the internet.
2. Wow! There (is / are) a lot of people in the station today!
3. There (was / were) some noise in the cafe, which made it difficult for me to study.
4. There (wasn't / weren't) many university options available to me.
5. Why (is / are) there so many bottles of milk in the fridge?

B (　　) 内の最も適切な語句を選び、英文を完成しなさい。

1. There (is / was / were) a big lightning and thunder storm last night.
2. How many students (is / are / was) there in your class now?
3. There (is / were / will be) someone at the airport to meet you tomorrow morning.
4. There (are / will / have been) some strange fashion trends in the world lately.
5. There (isn't / will / won't) be anyone in the company, because everyone will have gone home.

C 空所に are / was / isn't / wasn't / weren't のどれかに続く語句を組み合わせて、英文を完成しなさい。

a long line	a lot of food	~~many flowers~~	many tourists	much traffic	only ten

e.g. This garden is beautiful. There are many flowers blooming in it.

1. The road is almost empty. It's a holiday, so there ____________________.
2. I am riding on a bus. There ____________________ passengers right now.
3. We didn't have enough to eat. There ____________________ at the party last night.
4. When we got to the concert hall, there ____________________ at the entrance.
5. There ____________________ who visited this temple five years ago, although there are a lot of visitors these days.

D 前半に続く後半を (a) ～ (d) から選び、英文を完成しなさい。

1. There are a variety of _____.
2. There was a long wait before _____.
3. There will always be another _____.
4. There are twenty candles _____.

(a) opportunity for you to take the driver's test
(b) on his birthday cake
(c) our luggage arrived at the baggage claim
(d) unique sites we can visit while in Kyoto

6 Writing

A 日本語に合うように、(　　) 内の語句を並べ替えなさい。

1. In the 1890s at Madison Square Garden in New York, Nikola Tesla (a radio-controlled / could / he / how / move / off / showed) boat.
ニコラ・テスラは1890年代にニューヨークのマディソン・スクエア・ガーデンで、無線操縦のボートをどのように動せるか披露しました。

2. Before remotes were invented, TV watchers had to get up and (change / go to / rotating / the channel / their television sets / to / using) dials.
リモコンが発明される前、テレビ視聴者は回転ダイヤルを使ってチャンネルを変えるために、立ち上がってテレビ受像機まで行かなければなりませんでした。

B 次の質問に、(　　) 内の語句を使って答えなさい。

1. What kind of television programs do you watch? Why do you like them?
(enjoy watching variety shows / funny and entertaining)

2. Nowadays, more people watch streaming programs and fewer people watch TV. Do you think this trend will continue? Why or why not?
(continue to be popular / choose what they want)

Grammar Spotlight

▶There 構文

「～がある、～がいる」というように、何かの存在を表す場合に使う表現です。

1. There+be 動詞 [...] の使い方

there は形式的な主語で、[...] が意味上の主語にあたります。

There **is** a new recycled clothing **store** near here.
There **are** some popular **restaurants** on this shopping street.
There **was** a lot of **fruit** on the table.
There **were** many **things** to play in the park.

2. There 構文の否定文、疑問文、未来形

There **is not** a **car** on the street.
There **are no** **parking lots** around here.
There **wasn't** any **information** about the accident.
There **weren't** a lot of **people** in the room.
Are there any **questions**?
Was there a lot of **food** at the party?
There **will be** a **meeting** tomorrow.

Unit 6
Why Do ATM PINs Have Only Four Numbers?

▶ **articles / nouns**

銀行口座から現金を引き出す方法を考えていたATMの発明者が、暗証番号（PIN）として最初に思いついたのは6桁の番号でした。では、なぜ金融機関では4桁の数字が世界的に最もよく使われるようになったのでしょうか。

Warm-up

次の質問に英語で答えなさい。

1. How old were you when you got your first bank card?
2. What are some ways to choose a good PIN or password?

1 Vocabulary

英文の（　　）に入れる最も適切な単語を語群より選び、(A)～(J)で答えなさい。

(A) confirm	(B) complicated	(C) digit	(D) identification	(E) keypad
(F) password	(G) pattern	(H) personal	(I) remember	(J) secret

1. Don't ask how old she is. That is (　　) information.
2. He showed the police officer his (　　) — his driver's license and his school ID card.
3. You have to enter your password twice because the card company wants to (　　) that it is the right password.
4. If I tell you a (　　), you must promise not to tell anyone else.
5. Jerry was a little sad because his friends did not (　　) his birthday.
6. Did you know you can use a (　　) for a password? Some people's passwords are just triangles and stars.
7. You can enter your name by using the letters on the (　　) or touching the screen.
8. I made a mistake. The last (　　) of my PIN is 6, not 9.
9. To be safe, it is important that you change your (　　) every few months.
10. The lecture was quite (　　). There was too much information, and the topic was difficult to understand.

2 Reading

17

Personal Identification Numbers, or PINs, are an essential part of our lives today. For example, we use them to protect our personal information when we go to the bank. PINs also help card companies confirm our identity. They are like the passwords we use on websites. Website passwords are often long and complicated. Although our PINs are just as important as our internet passwords, they are only four digits long! Why are there only four numbers in our personal identification numbers?

When automated teller machines, or ATMs, were invented in 1967, banks needed a way to protect people's money and identity. So John Adrian Shepherd-Barron, the inventor of the ATM, decided that ATM users should have secret identification numbers. Originally, he wanted to use six numbers. But his wife, Caroline, didn't like the idea. She said that six numbers were too much to remember. She could only remember four. This is the reason why we have four-digit personal identification numbers today.

But some banks still require six-digit personal identification numbers. Unfortunately, customers often forget their PINs, especially if they are six digits long. That's why six-digit PINs have not really caught on.

Notes　**Personal Identification Number (= PIN)**「暗証番号」　**four digits long**「４桁の長さ」
automated teller machine (= ATM)「現金自動預け払い機」　**catch on**「流行する」

Reading Comprehension

A True or False

次の英文が本文の内容と一致する場合は T、一致しない場合は F を選びなさい。

1. PINs help protect users' personal information. [T F]
2. The wife of the inventor of the ATM preferred four-digit PINs because they were easy to remember. [T F]
3. Nowadays, all banks require customers to have four-digit PINs. [T F]

B Skimming and Scanning

本文の内容について、最も適切な答えや語句を (A) ～ (C) から選びなさい。

1. When were ATMs invented?
   (A) In the 1960s　(B) In the 1970s　(C) In the 1980s
2. John Adrian Shepherd-Barron first suggested using _____ numbers for PINs.
   (A) 4　(B) 6　(C) 8
3. Why haven't six-digit PINs caught on at banks?
   (A) Banks don't accept them.
   (B) Customers find them too easy to forget.
   (C) They are too easy to remember.

3 Conversation

A Listen and Write

18

次の会話を聞いて、(　　) に単語を書きなさい。

W: May I help you?
M: I'm sorry, but I [1](　　　　　　) my password.
W: No problem. Do you have two [2](　　　　　　) of identification?
M: I have a bank card and a credit card.
W: Do you have any ID with your [3](　　　　　　) on it?
M: Is my driver's [4](　　　　　　) okay?
W: Of course.

B Listen and Choose

19

質問を聞いて、(　　) に単語を書き、最も適切な応答を (A) ～ (C) から選びなさい。

1. (　　　　) (　　　　) the man (　　　　)?
(A) His credit card　(B) His password　(C) His wallet

2. What (　　　　) (　　　　) identification does the woman (　　　　) (　　　　) (　　　　)?
(A) A company ID　(B) A photo ID　(C) A school ID

Notes　**company ID**「社員証」　**photo ID**「顔写真付きの身分証明書」　**school ID**「学生証」

4 Text Completion

次の文章を読んで、空所に入れる最も適切なものを (A) ～ (C) から選びなさい。

HOW TO CHOOSE A GOOD PIN

(a) Don't choose numbers that are in a simple pattern. (for example, 0000, 1234)
(b) Don't choose numbers that are important to you (for example, your birthday, your telephone number)
(c) Don't tell your personal identification number to people you do not know.
(d) Don't use the same personal identification for your __1__ cards.
(e) Use the letters on the keypad. Each number also has letters. Use the numbers to create a word. (e.g. "WORD" is __2__ .)

2: ABC　3: DEF　4: GHI　5:JKL　6: MNO　7: PQRS　8: TUV　9: WXYZ

(f) Use a date __3__ is important to you and add 1 to each number. For example, if you were born on May 28th (05/28), you can add 1 to each number and use 1639 for your PIN.

1. (A) another　(B) other　(C) others
2. (A) 2679　(B) 9073　(C) 9673
3. (A) that　(B) what　(C) where

5 Grammar

A (　　) 内の適切な語句を選び、英文を完成しなさい。

1. It is difficult to find a (job / work) right now.
2. I would like to give you some (advice / advices) about your upcoming interview.
3. Sam works for a charity organization that gives food to (a poor / the poor).
4. Beth bought (a new computer / new computer) yesterday.
5. The coffee is in (cupboard / the cupboard) above the sink.
6. Students seem to have more and more (homework / homeworks) nowadays.
7. To stay safe, hockey players need some special (equipment / equipments).
8. There are a few (strawberry / strawberries) in the fridge.

B (　　) に a / an, the, X (冠詞不要の場合) を入れて、英文を完成しなさい。

1. Excuse me. Is there (　　) bank near here?
2. When I have time, I love to relax and watch (　　) sunset.
3. If the juice is too sour, you can add (　　) sugar.
4. The new president seems to be (　　) honest man.
5. Do you remember John's new dog? Well, (　　) dog ran away last weekend.
6. Do you think (　　) Greek is difficult to learn?
7. Could you tell me (　　) meaning of this sentence?
8. We had (　　) difficult biology test today. I hope I did well.

C 空所に入れる名詞を語群から選び、適切な形に変えて英文を完成しなさい。

child	dish	fruit	glass	hair

1. Sarah makes several tasty ________________ for dinner every day.
2. My brother drinks two ________________ of milk before breakfast.
3. Only a few ________________ are playing in the neighborhood park right now.
4. Tina uses four different dried ________________ to make her famous fruitcake.
5. My father is getting a few gray ________________ already, but he's only 40!

D 前半に続く後半を (a) ～ (d) から選び、英文を完成しなさい。

1. I used to read British newspapers _____.
2. Sometimes, I have trouble _____.
3. It is important for you to keep _____.
4. If you enter the wrong PIN three times in _____.

(a) a row, the card will get blocked
(b) to improve my English vocabulary
(c) remembering my password
(d) your personal identification number a secret

6 Writing

A 日本語に合うように、(　　) 内の語句を並べ替えなさい。

1. ATM PINs are four digits long, as (numbers / of / string / that / the inventor's / the longest / was) wife could remember.
ATM の暗証番号は 4 桁の長さです。それが、発明家の妻が覚えることができた最も長い数字列だったからです。

2. As ATMs became more common, it (four-digit PINs / became / before / long / standard / the world / wasn't).
ATM がより一般的になったので、4 桁の暗証番号が世界の標準になるのにそれほど時間はかかりませんでした。

B 次の質問に、(　　) 内の語句を使って答えなさい。

1. Have you ever forgotten your ATM PIN or smartphone password? What happened?
(Once, I forgot / It was locked / to unlock)

2. Some people are concerned about shopping online because they feel it is not safe. Do you agree or disagree with them?
(is not 100% safe / protect your privacy)

Grammar Spotlight

▶冠詞

冠詞は名詞を修飾して、「特定されていないもの」と「特定されたもの」を区別します。

1. 不定冠詞 a / an

初めて話題に上る、数えられる単数名詞に付けます。

Do you live in **a** dormitory or **an** apartment?
It is **an** ad for **an** upcoming concert.

2. 定冠詞 the

可算・不可算、単数・複数を問わず名詞の前に付き、特定のものを表します。

The woman I saw at **the** supermarket was my boss.

状況から特定性が明らかな場合

Please pass me **the** salt.

限定用法の形容詞の最上級

The smallest unit of matter is the atom.

▶名詞

名詞は人や物、事柄を表し、数えられる名詞と数えられない名詞があります。

1. 数えられる名詞（可算名詞）

普通名詞 (bicycle, desk, room, etc.)

・不定冠詞 (a / an)、定冠詞 (the) が付くか、または複数形になります。

Is there a **bank** nearby?
Eric uses a **laptop** to take **notes** in class.
The **dictionaries** on the **shelf** are often used these days.

集合名詞 (audience, family, police, etc.)

The **family** are all very talented.
The **police** are on the scene.

2. 数えられない名詞（不可算名詞）

固有名詞 (Italy, Wilson, etc.)、物質名詞 (coffee, salt, etc.)、抽象名詞 (information, honesty, etc.)

・advice, baggage, beer, furniture, health, knowledge, news, truth などは不可算名詞で、不定冠詞 (a / an) を付けたり複数形にしたりしません。

× Would you give me some **advices** about the SAT exam?
○ Would you give me some **advice** about the SAT exam?

× I have **a good news**.
○ I have **good news**.

3. 数えられない名詞の数え方

Allison drank **two glasses of** juice.

・a bottle of wine, a cup of coffee, a pair of glasses, a piece of cake, a pint of milk, a sheet of paper, etc.

Unit 7
Why Are Pencils Yellow?

▶infinitives / gerunds

鉛筆と言えば何色をイメージしますか。茶色や緑色を想像する人もいるかもしれませんが、アメリカでは鉛筆のスタンダードカラーは黄色で、しかも消しゴム付きです。鉛筆メーカーはなぜ、商品のイメージアップのために黄色を使ったのでしょうか。

Warm-up

次の質問に英語で答えなさい。

1. What is your favorite color? Why do you like it?
2. Do you like to write with a pencil or pen? Why?

1 Vocabulary

英文の（　　）に入れる最も適切な単語を語群より選び、(A) ～ (J) で答えなさい。

(A) actually	(B) decorate	(C) materials	(D) mechanical	(E) messy
(F) originally	(G) print	(H) royalty	(I) skill	(J) superior

1. My son likes to (　　) his bedroom walls with posters of superheroes and villains.
2. Small amounts of gold, copper, and other precious (　　) are all found inside your computer.
3. Japanese pencils are (　　) to those made in other countries. They not only have better lead, but better erasers, too.
4. If you are a member of Queen Elizabeth's family, even if you are only a distant cousin, you are considered (　　).
5. I am (　　) from Chicago, Illinois, but now I live permanently in London.
6. I thought the final exam would be much more difficult, but (　　) it was quite easy, and I aced it.
7. Sign language is one (　　) I really want to learn so I can communicate with people who have hearing problems.
8. Look at how (　　) your room is. There are books, papers, food wrappers, and empty drink cartons all over the floor. Clean it up now!
9. Our house in Okayama has an old-fashioned (　　) water pump. We have to pump all our water from the well by hand.
10. When you fill out this form, make sure you (　　) all your letters very neatly so that people can easily read it.

2 Reading

20

Nowadays, you can find pencils in all sorts of different colors and shapes. Originally, most pencils were colored yellow. You can still find yellow pencils in schools, offices, and people's homes. Do you know why pencils are colored yellow? Well, the reason might surprise you.

Some people think it's because yellow pencils are easy to find on a messy desk. Actually, pencils have been colored yellow since the 1890s. Back then, pencil leads were made using a special material called graphite. The best graphite in the world came from China. Pencil manufactures wanted their customers to know that they used superior Chinese graphite for their pencils. So they started coloring their pencils yellow, which, in China, is the color of royalty and respect.

Although some people still use traditional yellow pencils, most people today prefer to use mechanical pencils or colorful pencils decorated with their favorite anime or superhero characters. Few people remember that yellow pencils once meant that the pencils had a special meaning.

Notes **messy desk**「散らかったデスク」 **lead**「芯」 **superior Chinese graphite**「良質な中国産黒鉛」 **mechanical pencil**「シャーペン」

Reading Comprehension

A True or False

次の英文が本文の内容と一致する場合は T、一致しない場合は F を選びなさい。

1. Nobody thinks yellow pencils are easy to find. [**T F**]
2. Back in the 1890s, most pencils were colored yellow. [**T F**]
3. Nowadays, most people still think yellow pencils are easier to use than mechanical pencils. [**T F**]

B Skimming and Scanning

本文の内容について、空所に入れる最も適切な語句を (A) ～ (C) から選びなさい。

1. In the past, the best lead for pencils came from _____.
   (A) Canada (B) China (C) the U.K.
2. In China, the color yellow stands for _____.
   (A) royalty and respect (B) sunshine (C) superior quality
3. Nowadays, yellow pencils are _____ they once were.
   (A) less expensive than
   (B) more common than
   (C) not as popular as

3 Conversation

A Listen and Write

21

次の会話を聞いて、(　　) に単語を書きなさい。

W: May I [1](　　　　　　　) your pen?
M: Sure. Here you go.
W: Wow! This is a nice pen. It is so easy to [2](　　　　　　　) with.
M: Thanks! I just [3](　　　　　　　) it. It's much better than my old pen.
W: It looks more [4](　　　　　　　), too.
M: Hahaha. Yeah. A little.

B Listen and Choose

22

質問を聞いて、(　　) に単語を書き、最も適切な応答を (A) ～ (C) から選びなさい。

1. (　　　　　　) does the woman (　　　　　　) the man (　　　　　　)?
(A) To give her back her pencil
(B) To help her write something
(C) To lend her a pen

2. (　　　　　　) does the woman (　　　　　　) the (　　　　　　) (　　　　　　)?
(A) It is very easy to write with.
(B) It looks more expensive than her own pen.
(C) It is brand new.

Notes　**here you go**「どうぞ」　**brand new**「新品の」

4 Text Completion

次の文章を読んで、空所に入れる最も適切なものを (A) ～ (C) から選びなさい。

Because more students are using computers, they spend less and less time ___1___ their handwriting. In many North American schools, students only learn how to print letters. People say that there is no need ___2___ writing because in the future, people will enter everything they need to write on tablets or laptops. Other people say that writing is still an important skill because it helps us ___3___. What do you think?

1. (A) practice　(B) practicing　(C) to practice
2. (A) practice　(B) practicing　(C) to practice
3. (A) have some trouble
(B) pass tests more easily
(C) understand and remember information better

5 Grammar

A (　　) 内の適切な語句を選び、英文を完成しなさい。

1. I really enjoyed (to attend / attending) the concert with you.
2. My parents don't think it is a good idea (to watch / watching) too much TV before bed.
3. Would you mind (to turn / turning) off the TV, please?
4. Derek hopes (to go / going) camping next weekend.
5. My housemates and I go (shopping / to shop) for groceries on Sunday.

B (　　) 内の最も適切なものを選び、英文を完成しなさい。

1. Jimmy likes (taking / to take / どちらも可) photographs of interesting buildings.
2. Please remember (locking / to lock / どちらも可) the door when you go out.
3. It started (raining / to rain / どちらも可) early this morning.
4. The doctor advised Martha (exercising / to exercise / どちらも可) more.
5. Mary began (studying / to study / どちらも可) violin at the age of three.
6. We are considering (to visit / visiting / どちらも可) several temples in Kyoto.
7. Sorry I'm late. I stopped (buying / to buy / どちらも可) some cake at the cake shop on 4th Avenue.

C 空所に入れる語を語群より選び、不定詞か動名詞にして英文を完成しなさい。

clean	eat	go	read	travel

1. Sally wants to become better at ________________ English, so she is taking a literature class.
2. Next year, David plans ________________ around Europe.
3. You can go out with your friends after you finish ________________ the room.
4. I stopped ________________ fast food. My doctor told me to lose some weight!
5. Natalie is looking forward to ________________ to university in the fall.

D 前半に続く後半を (a) ～ (d) から選び、英文を完成しなさい。

1. A friend of mine in Vancouver invited me _____.
2. Regina prefers exercising at home to _____.
3. James brought some flowers to _____.
4. We had so much fun that we decided _____.

(a) say thanks to his girlfriend
(b) to stay at the resort for two more days
(c) to visit her when I go to Canada
(d) working out at the fitness center

6 Writing

A 日本語に合うように、(　　) 内の語句を並べ替えなさい。

1. American pencil makers wanted (contained / people / show / that / the best / their pencils / to) graphite from China.
アメリカの鉛筆メーカーは、鉛筆に中国産の極上の黒鉛が入っていることを人々に示したいと思いました。

2. Yellow is a royal color in China, so American pencil makers (associate / colored / their pencils / them / to / with / yellow) China.
黄色は中国では皇族の色なので、アメリカの鉛筆メーカーは鉛筆を中国と関連づけるために黄色に塗りました。

B 次の質問に、(　　) 内の語句を使って答えなさい。

1. What color has special meaning or significance to you?
(I like shades of / it symbolizes)

2. Some people say that students should spend more time learning how to write in cursive. Others say it is not necessary because the world is becoming digital. What do you think?
(made us write / help us improve)

Grammar Spotlight

▶不定詞

「to＋動詞の原形」を不定詞と言います。

動詞に to を付けることで、名詞・形容詞・副詞の働きをします。

To discover a new color someday is Mark's dream.「～すること」
＜名詞的用法＞

Jennifer has an assignment **to hand in** today.「～すべき」
＜形容詞的用法＞

Edward went to college **to study** economics.「～するために」
＜副詞的用法＞

▶動名詞

動詞の原形に -ing を付けた形を動名詞と言います。

主語・補語・目的語・前置詞の目的語の働きをします。

Finding information on the internet is very efficient.　＜主語＞

The topic of today's discussion is **studying** abroad.　＜補語＞

Young people love **using** social media.　＜目的語＞

I'm looking forward to **seeing** you next Sunday.　＜前置詞の目的語＞

▶間違いやすい表現

1. 不定詞のみを目的語に取る動詞、動名詞のみを目的語にとる動詞

不定詞：afford, agree, claim, decide, plan, refuse, want, wish, etc.
動名詞：avoid, enjoy, deny, finish, give up, mind, miss, resist, etc.

Lillian **wants to buy** a pair of new jeans.
Tony has just **finished reading** the newspaper.

2. 不定詞と動名詞の両方を取り、意味が同じ動詞：like, love, start, begin など

Sally **likes reading [to read]** in her spare time.
His girlfriend doesn't **like shopping [to shop]**.

3. 不定詞と動名詞で意味が異なる動詞：forget, remember, regret, stop など

Alan **remembers to do** the work.「～するのを覚えている」
Bill **remembers doing** the work.「～したことを覚えている」

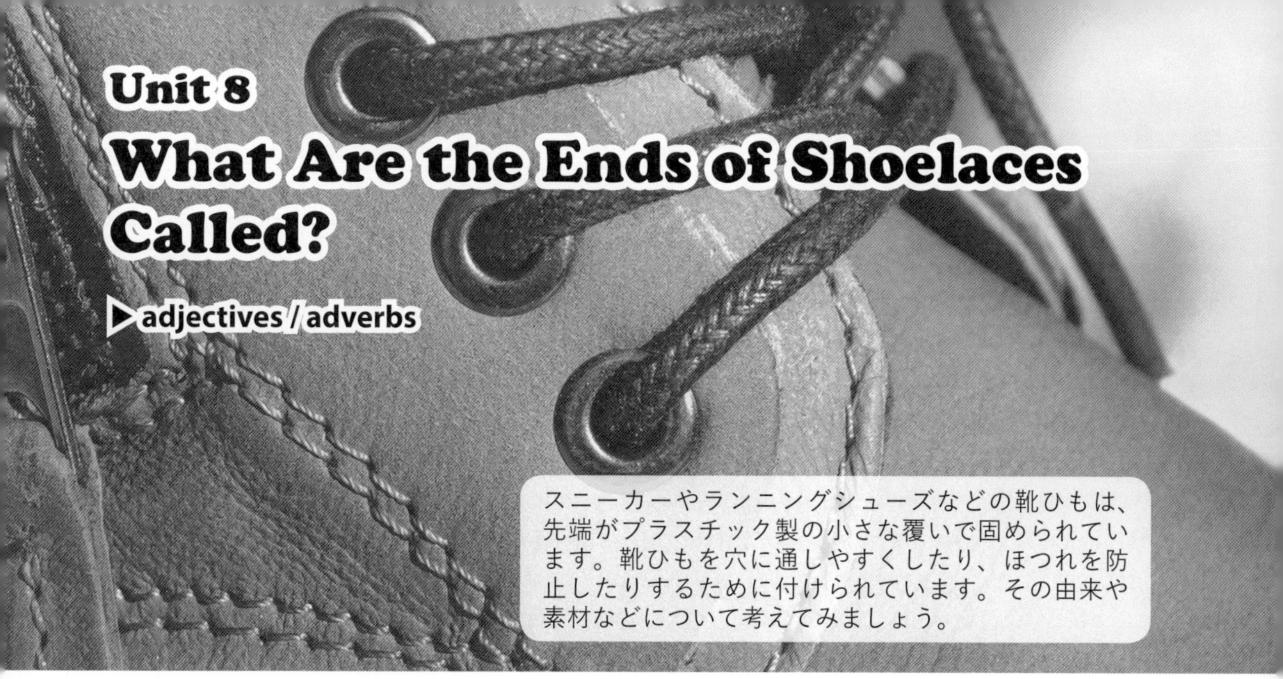

Unit 8
What Are the Ends of Shoelaces Called?

▶adjectives / adverbs

スニーカーやランニングシューズなどの靴ひもは、先端がプラスチック製の小さな覆いで固められています。靴ひもを穴に通しやすくしたり、ほつれを防止したりするために付けられています。その由来や素材などについて考えてみましょう。

Warm-up

次の質問に英語で答えなさい。

1. What kind of shoes do you like to wear everyday? Why?
2. Do you have shoes that you only use for a certain special activity?

1 Vocabulary

英文の（　　）に入れる最も適切な単語を語群より選び、(A) ～ (J) で答えなさい。

(A) automatically	(B) chemicals	(C) cover	(D) fancy	(E) functional
(F) heartrate	(G) military	(H) needle	(I) sensor	(J) shoelaces

1. Don't forget to close the (　　) on the copy machine. Otherwise, the glass will get dirty.
2. He checked his (　　) after running, and saw that his heart was beating 170 times a minute.
3. This beautiful bowl is (　　). It can be used for many things.
4. In some countries, young people must serve time in the (　　): either the army or the navy.
5. Farmers use (　　) to kill harmful insects that would destroy their crops.
6. Your (　　) are untied. You had better stop and tie them, or you might trip.
7. Some cars today have a (　　) that can tell you when you are too close to the car in front of you.
8. Some latest model cars move (　　). They don't need a driver.
9. A button fell off my shirt. Do you have a (　　) and some thread so I can sew it back on?
10. Wow! What a (　　) party! Everyone is wearing beautiful dresses and tuxedoes!

2 Reading

23

Look at your shoes. Do you see little plastic covers on the ends of your shoelaces? Do you know what they are called? Do you know what they are for?

Those little plastic covers or sheaths are called “aglets.” The name comes from an Old French word, *aguillet*, which means “needle” or “pin.” Aglets keep the strings in your shoelaces together so that the laces don’t unravel or come apart.

Originally, aglets were made of glass, metal, or stone. In ancient Rome, wealthy people made their aglets from precious metals like gold and silver. Some people also used aglets to decorate pieces of string, curtain cords, and the ribbons on fancy dresses as well as military uniforms.

So, what are aglets for? Because of the shape and hardness of aglets, it is easier to thread the shoelaces through the holes in our shoes. Today, of course, most aglets are made of plastic. Special machines first wrap the plastic around the shoelaces. Heat or chemicals are then used to stick the plastic and shoelace together. Nowadays, aglets are more functional than fashionable, although some do come in different colors and patterns.

Notes **aglet**「アグレット」靴ひも先金具 **keep ... together**「～を束ねる」 **unravel**「ほぐれる」 **precious metal**「貴金属」 **curtain cord**「カーテンのひも」 **military uniform**「軍服」 **thread ... through**「…を～に通す」

Reading Comprehension

A True or False

次の英文が本文の内容と一致する場合は T、一致しない場合は F を選びなさい。

1. Aglets keep the strings in shoelaces from coming apart. [T F]
2. Wealthy Romans' aglets were quite fancy. [T F]
3. Aglets have always been purely fashionable. [T F]

B Skimming and Scanning

本文の内容について、空所に入れる最も適切な語句を (A) ～ (C) から選びなさい。

1. Aglet comes from a word that means “needle” or “pin.” This word comes from _____.
   (A) Old English (B) Old French (C) Old Roman
2. Aglets were originally made from _____.
   (A) glass, metal, or stone (B) gold and silver (C) wood
3. The plastic and the string are wrapped together by _____.
   (A) hand (B) robots (C) special machines

3 Conversation

A Listen and Write

24

次の会話を聞いて、(　　) に単語を書きなさい。

W: Are you [1] (　　　　　　) to go for a run!
M: I sure am. [2] (　　　　　　) go!
W: Wait a second!
M: [3] (　　　　　　) me?
W: Your shoelaces are [4] (　　　　　　).
M: What? Oh! Thanks! OK, now I'm ready.

B Listen and Choose

25

質問を聞いて、(　　) に単語を書き、最も適切な応答を (A) ～ (C) から選びなさい。

1. Why did the woman (　　　　　　) the man (　　　　) (　　　　　　)?
(A) He was running too fast.
(B) His shoelaces were untied.
(C) She wanted to ask him a question.

2. (　　　　　　) (　　　　　　) the man and woman probably (　　　　) (　　　　　　)?
(A) Go running
(B) Go shopping for shoelaces
(C) Wait for a friend to join them

Notes **go for a run**「ひと走りする」 **wait a second**「ちょっと待って」

4 Text Completion

次の文章を読んで、空所に入れる最も適切なものを (A) ～ (C) から選びなさい。

Soon, it will be possible to wear shoes that have computers in them! __1__ new technology, many companies can make shoes smarter. For example, some companies are putting __2__ sensors into running shoes. These sensors can measure the heartrate, distance, and speed of athletes. One company has created a smart shoe that even knows when you put your foot in the shoe. __3__, the shoe automatically ties the laces!

1. (A) Although　　(B) As for　　(C) Thanks to
2. (A) smart　　(B) smarten　　(C) smartly
3. (A) As soon as you put your foot inside
(B) If you do not put your shoe on
(C) When someone touches your shoe

5 Grammar

A (　　) 内の適切なものを選び、英文を完成しなさい。

1. I always feel (happy / happily) when I hear about someone's good deed.
2. If you eat too (quick / quickly), you will give yourself a stomachache.
3. I want to learn how to sing as (beautiful / beautifully) as an opera singer.
4. Johnny stayed up (late / lately) last night playing a new game.
5. (Fortunate / Fortunately), we arrived at the stadium just in time for the first pitch.

B 各組の見出しの単語を適切な形 (形容詞・副詞) にして空所に書き、英文を完成しなさい。

e.g. (a) He ran **quickly** to the store.　(b) Jed is a **quick** runner.

1. angry
(a) Mr. Baker's ______________ dog barked at the dog next door.
(b) The dog barked ______________ at the paper delivery boy.

2. careful
(a) The nurse wrapped the bandages ______________ around the patient's head.
(b) Dr. Smith was ______________ not to cause the patient any pain.

3. nervous
(a) Sally is always ______________ when she talks in front of people.
(b) Sally fumbled ______________ with the script for her speech.

4. quiet
(a) Shhh! This is a ______________ study area.
(b) Shhh! You should study ______________ here in the library.

5. serious
(a) Tom trains very ______________ for the marathon.
(b) Tom is a ______________ athlete who trains very hard.

C (　　) に入れる単語を語群から選び、形容詞か副詞に変えて、英文を完成しなさい。

comfort	expense	noise	origin	week

1. Beth couldn't sleep well because it was (　　　　　　) outside her hotel room.
2. I've just bought a really nice, (　　　　　　) watch. I wanted to reward myself for passing the exam.
3. Our office meetings are held (　　　　　　) on Friday mornings.
4. The colors in the copy are more vivid than those in the (　　　　　　) painting.
5. Paul is sitting (　　　　　　) on the sofa, drinking coffee, and watching a documentary.

D 前半に続く後半を (a) ～ (d) から選び、英文を完成しなさい。

1. You need to complete the form very _____.
2. Sally needed to work fast so she _____.
3. Wearing shoes that don't fit properly _____.
4. No matter how busy I am, I try to eat _____.

(a) can lead to foot problems
(b) carefully without making any mistakes
(c) healthy and exercise every day
(d) could finish the project on time

6 Writing

A 日本語に合うように、(　　) 内の語句を並べ替えなさい。

1. The word "aglet" refers to the little plastic (around / casing / is / of / placed / that / the end) a shoelace.
「アグレット」という語は、靴ひもの端に巻きつけられている小さなプラスチックの覆いのことを言います。

2. The little plastic tip makes (easier / it / the holes / the shoelace / thread / through / to).
小さなプラスチックの先端は、穴に靴ひもを通すことをより簡単にします。

B 次の質問に、(　　) 内の語句を使って答えなさい。

1. What special equipment do you use to stay healthy? What fitness equipment would you like to try?
(a step tracker / monitor my health)

2. These days, many people use wearable technology like smart watches and heart monitors. Some people are concerned that these devices invade their privacy. What do you think?
(worry about my privacy / today's technology / personal information)

Grammar Spotlight

▶形容詞

1. 限定用法：名詞を修飾して名詞の意味を限定します。

Catherine always wears a **nice outfit**.
This **hybrid car** is economical.
I'd like to drink **something cold**.
・something のように -thing で終わる語の場合は形容詞を後ろに置きます。

2. 叙述用法：文中で補語の働きをします。

Online shopping is **convenient** for customers.
＜形容詞が主格補語：S+V+C ＞
I found him **honest**.　＜形容詞が目的格補語：S+V+O+C ＞

▶副詞

動詞・形容詞・副詞・文全体を修飾します。

Daniel **clearly remembers** his elementary school graduation ceremony.　＜動詞を修飾＞
Laura is **very careful** when she chooses her dresses.　＜形容詞を修飾＞
Jessica is cooking **so happily**.　＜副詞を修飾＞
Fortunately, the weather is excellent for hiking.　＜文全体を修飾＞

副詞の作り方

・形容詞の語尾に -ly
quick → quickly　extreme → extremely　slow → slowly

・形容詞の語尾の y を i に変えて -ly
easy → easily　happy → happily　lucky → luckily

・-able, -ible, -le は、語尾の e を取って -y
probable → probably　terrible → terribly　gentle → gently

・副詞と形容詞が同じもの
early, fast, hard, high, late, etc.

Unit 9

Why Are Gym Shoes Called "Sneakers"?

▶ comparative forms

カジュアルスタイルの足元に欠かせないのがスニーカーです。若者のファッションを演出してくれるスニーカーは、1970 年代後半にアメリカで一気に爆発的な人気を得ました。スニーカーの由来について考えてみましょう。

Warm-up

次の質問に英語で答えなさい。

1. What do you think of the shoes in the photo above? Would you wear shoes like them? Why or why not?
2. How many pairs of shoes do you have? What do you use each pair for?

1 Vocabulary

英文の（　　）に入れる最も適切な単語を語群より選び、(A) 〜 (J) で答えなさい。

(A) cautiously	(B) conscious	(C) criminals	(D) industry	(E) market
(F) nurse	(G) own	(H) prison	(I) soles	(J) trend

1. A: Do you (　　) a car?
   B: No, I prefer to take public transportation.
2. It was snowing hard, so I had to drive very (　　).
3. The (　　) of my shoes are almost worn off. I need to get some new shoes.
4. After the (　　) stole money, they all fled the country.
5. My mother works as a (　　) on the hospital's COVID-19 ward.
6. The art thief spent ten years in (　　) for stealing an Edward Hopper painting.
7. Every year, there's a hot new (　　). This year, the latest fad is recording short videos of yourself dancing to pop songs.
8. People today are becoming more (　　) of the need to protect the environment.
9. The (　　) for health food is growing as more people are demanding products with less fat and sugar and fewer calories.
10. The service (　　) is becoming increasingly automated. Jobs like sales clerks and information assistants are done over by robots.

2 Reading 26

Almost everyone owns at least one pair of running shoes. We use them all the time to play sports, for our daily runs or walks, or just because they are so comfortable to go shopping or to commute in. Running shoes go by lots of different names—kicks, runners, gym shoes, and daps. But in America, they are commonly called "sneakers."

The modern English word "sneak" comes from an Old English word, *snican*, which means "to move quietly and cautiously." Gradually, the word evolved into "sneak," and people who walked quietly because they didn't want to be heard were said to be "sneaking around." So how did running shoes come to be called sneakers?

In the past, the soles of most shoes were made of wood or hard leather. Everywhere people went, they "clomped around" and made a lot of noise. But around 1830, the soles of some shoes started being made from rubber. This enabled people to walk around much more quietly. As you can imagine, thieves and other criminals loved these "sneaky" shoes. But so did others—like nurses and prison guards, for example—who needed to walk quietly at their work.

These quieter, more comfortable rubber-soled shoes caught on, as did the word "sneakers" to describe them. Interestingly, although Americans call them sneakers, people in the U.K. call them "trainers." I wonder why. Could it be that British people are more health conscious?

Notes **all the time**「いつも」 **go by**「(通称など)を使う」 **commute**「通勤(通学)する」 **Old English**「古英語」 **sneak around**「こそこそ歩く」 **clomp around**「ドタドタと歩く」 **prison guard**「刑務官」

Reading Comprehension

A True or False

次の英文が本文の内容と一致する場合は T、一致しない場合は F を選びなさい。

1. "Running shoes" go by many different names. [T F]
2. Originally, the soles of all shoes were made from metal. [T F]
3. People liked "sneakers" because they could work more quietly in them. [T F]

B Skimming and Scanning

本文の内容について、空所に入れる最も適切な語句を (A) ～ (C) から選びなさい。

1. The word "sneakers" comes from an Old English word that means _____.
   (A) to train hard (B) to walk carefully (C) to walk quickly
2. Once the soles of shoes were made from rubber, people could _____.
   (A) run more quickly (B) train more regularly (C) walk more quietly

3. People in England often call running shoes _____.
(A) daps (B) runners (C) trainers

3 Conversation

A Listen and Write 27

次の会話を聞いて、(　　) に単語を書きなさい。

W: Hi. How may I help you?
M: I'm [1](　　　　　　　) for a new pair of sneakers.
W: What will you [2](　　　　　) them for?
M: I want to wear them [3](　　　　　　　) when I hang out with friends.
W: Okay. Do you have a [4](　　　　　　　) brand or color?
M: Not really, but maybe something in purple.

B Listen and Choose 28

質問を聞いて、(　　) に単語を書き、最も適切な応答を (A) ～ (C) から選びなさい。

1. (　　　　　) is the man (　　　　　　　) (　　　　　)?
(A) A clerk to help him (B) Friends to hang out with (C) Shoes to wear

2. (　　　　　　　) is the conversation probably (　　　　　　　) (　　　　　　)?
(A) At a store (B) In a fitness center (C) In a recycle shop

Notes **hang out with**「～と出かけて遊ぶ」 **not really**「そうでもない」

4 Text Completion

次の文章を読んで、空所に入れる最も適切なものを (A) ～ (C) から選びなさい。

Recently, people are wearing sportswear not only to the gym but also for all kinds of activities. Employees, both men and women, often wear sneakers at work. It is also common to wear exercise pants when people go shopping or eat out at a restaurant. This trend is becoming __1__, so clothing companies have created a new clothing style called "athleisure." As its name implies, athleisure clothing is used __2__. The athleisure market is one of the __3__ growing industries in North America.

1. (A) popularer (B) more popular (C) most popular
2. (A) by adult and children
(B) for both training and casual wear
(C) only by professional sports stars
3. (A) fast (B) faster (C) fastest

Notes **athleisure**「アスリジャー」athletic（アスレチック）と leisure（レジャー）を組み合わせた造語

5 Grammar

A (　　) 内の最も適切な語句を選び、英文を完成しなさい。

1. Who do you think is the (cute / cuter / cutest) boy in the band?
2. Trees closer to the mountain top are often (short / shorter / shortest) than those growing near the base.
3. Going to the beach is (fun / more fun / most fun) than studying math.
4. You can eat as (much / more / most) as you want.
5. Apples grow as (slow / slower / slowly) as oranges in this region.
6. This is the (delicious / more delicious / most delicious) steak I've ever eaten.
7. I can't keep up with her. She runs much (fast / faster / fastest) than I do.
8. Please get here as (soon / sooner / soonest) as possible.

B 同じ意味を表すように空所に入れる語句を書き、英文を完成しなさい。

1. Monica is not as friendly as her boyfriend.
= Monica's boyfriend is ＿＿＿＿＿＿＿＿＿＿ than she is.

2. The pub is noisier than the library.
= The library isn't as ＿＿＿＿＿＿＿＿ as the pub.

3. The last task wasn't as difficult as this one.
= This task is ＿＿＿＿＿＿＿＿＿＿＿ than the last one.

4. It's still hot, but it was hotter yesterday.
= It isn't as ＿＿＿＿＿＿＿＿ as it was yesterday.

5. Jason is smarter than any other student in the class.
= Jason is the ＿＿＿＿＿＿＿＿＿＿ of all students in the class.

C 空所に入れる単語を語群から選び、比較級に変えて、英文を完成しなさい。

big	carefully	easy	pretty	quickly

1. This new copier prints pages ＿＿＿＿＿＿＿＿＿＿ than the old one.
2. I want to buy a ＿＿＿＿＿＿＿＿＿＿ sweater. This one is too small.
3. The more flowers you grow, the ＿＿＿＿＿＿＿＿＿＿ your garden will be.
4. I found this assignment a little ＿＿＿＿＿＿＿＿＿＿ than the last one.
5. There are many mistakes in your report. You should write ＿＿＿＿＿＿＿＿＿＿ next time.

D 前半に続く後半を (a) ～ (d) から選び、英文を完成しなさい。

1. The sunrise I saw from the top of Mt. Fuji was _____.
2. Wearing sneakers is much more comfortable _____.
3. Eating out at fast-food restaurants is not as healthy _____.
4. Robots are being used more and more _____.

(a) as making your meals at home
(b) because they are cheaper and more dependable
(c) than wearing dress shoes
(d) the most beautiful sight I have ever seen

6 Writing

A 日本語に合うように、(　　) 内の語句を並べ替えなさい。

1. Sneakers originated in the 1800s. "Sneakers" is a more common (elsewhere / in / in America / is / it / term / than) the world, but the British call them "trainers."
スニーカーは1800年代に生まれました。「スニーカー」は世界のどの場所よりアメリカで一般的な言葉ですが、イギリス人はそれを「トレーナー」と呼びます。

2. Sneakers got their name because the rubber soles on the shoes enabled (making / on / others / people / sneak up / to / without) a sound.
スニーカーは靴のゴム底が、人々が音を立てずに他人にこっそり近づくことを可能にしたので、その名前がつきました。

B 次の質問に、(　　) 内の語句を使って答えなさい。

1. What kinds of shoes do you usually wear? Why do you wear them so often?
(I often wear [I occasionally put on] / more comfortable than)

2. Many businesses now allow employees to dress casually in the office. What do you think about that?
(I think casual wear / comfortable for / not look professional)

Grammar Spotlight

▶比較表現

比較表現は物事を比較する時に使い、原級・比較級・最上級の形があります。

1. 同等比較：as ＋形容詞・副詞の原級＋ as

Phil is **as diligent as** his colleagues.
Stella speaks Spanish **as fluently as** her brother.

2. 比較級：比較級＋ than

Mason cooks **better than** his wife does.
The bike is **more expensive than** I thought.

3. 最上級：the ＋最上級

Grace's design for athleisure shoes is **the best** of all.
Jenny is **the most reliable** person in the office.

4. 注意すべき比較表現

the + 比較級 , the + 比較級「…すればするほど、ますます～」
The sooner they leave, **the sooner** they can get there.

the + 比較級 + of the two「2つのうちより～の方」
Jenny is **the taller of the two**.

比較級・最上級の作り方

＜規則変化＞	原級	比較級	最上級
・原級に -er, -est	high	higher	highest
・語尾が -e は -r, -st	nice	nicer	nicest
・子音＋ y は y を i にして -er, -est	busy	busier	busiest
・短母音＋子音は子音を重ねて -er, -est	hot	hotter	hottest
・2音節以上の語は前に more, most	careful	more careful	most careful
less, least	polite	less polite	least polite
＜不規則変化＞	good	better	best
	bad	worse	worst
	little	less	least

Unit 10
Why Do We Drink So Much Coffee?

▶prepositions

アメリカ人はコーヒーを愛してやみません。日本では、コーヒーはブラックでという人もいますが、アメリカ人のほとんどはミルクや砂糖を入れます。人々がコーヒーを飲む理由や、コーヒー豆に関わる人たちについて考えてみましょう。

Warm-up

次の質問に英語で答えなさい。

1. How many cups of coffee do you drink each day?
2. Do you think it's important to know where your food and drinks come from? Why or why not?

1 Vocabulary

英文の（　　）に入れる最も適切な単語を語群より選び、(A) ～ (J) で答えなさい。

(A) billion	(B) climate	(C) commodity	(D) export	(E) grow
(F) harvest	(G) hybrid	(H) prevent	(I) resistant	(J) tap

1. A (　　) is equivalent to one thousand million in the U.S.
2. In some countries, people cannot drink the water that comes from the (　　), so they keep large bottles of purified water in the house.
3. Drinking green tea can help (　　) heart disease, diabetes, and even tooth decay.
4. The latest (　　) in the art world are NFTs, or digital artworks, which sell for surprisingly high prices.
5. Japan's largest (　　) is refined petroleum. It ranks 19th in the world at selling this product.
6. During pandemic lockdowns, many people started to (　　) their own vegetables out of necessity and as a hobby.
7. When the stalks of rice in the field turn yellow and start to bend towards the ground, it's time to (　　) the rice.
8. This quartz watch is 100 percent (　　) to water, which is why it is the #1 choice of professional divers.
9. The first (　　) vehicle—a small train that used both gas and electricity—was invented in 1889.
10. The latest United Nations report says that (　　) change, or global warming, is the greatest threat to the future of Planet Earth.

2 Reading

29

Billions of people the world over start their day off with a cup of coffee. Globally, people drink 500 billion cups of coffee each year. That's almost one and a half billion cups every single day! Coffee is America's most popular drink. In fact, Americans drink more coffee than they drink tap water.

Why do we drink so much coffee? For one thing, the caffeine in coffee gives us a boost of energy and keeps our minds sharp. Drinking coffee also has some health benefits. Scientists say it improves memory, controls weight, prevents diabetes, and even helps us live longer.

Where did coffee originate? An ancient legend says that an Ethiopian goat farmer named Kaldi noticed something strange. After his goats ate some berries from a certain tree, the goats became super energetic. Kaldi reported his discovery to a local monk, who made a drink from the berries. The drink made the monk energetic, too. Gradually, knowledge of the drink's amazing powers slowly spread throughout the Middle East, then to Europe, and finally around the globe.

Coffee is one of the world's most valuable commodities. It is grown in over 70 countries, and some of them are very poor. These countries depend on the income and jobs that the export of coffee provides. Unfortunately, for many reasons, climate change is making it more difficult to grow and harvest coffee. But scientists have developed hybrid coffee beans. These new types are more resistant to higher temperatures, pests, and disease.

Notes **billions of**「何十億もの」 **the world over**「世界中で」 **500 billion**「5千億」 **every single day**「毎日毎日」 **tap water**「水道水」 **boost of energy**「活力を高めること」 **the Middle East**「中東」 **valuable commodity**「貴重な産物」 **hybrid coffee bean**「ハイブリッドコーヒー豆」

Reading Comprehension

A True or False

次の英文が本文の内容と一致する場合は T、一致しない場合は F を選びなさい。

1. People around the world drink 500 million cups of coffee a day. [**T F**]

2. Coffee contains something called caffeine. [**T F**]

3. Climate change is having a negative effect on coffee growing. [**T F**]

B Skimming and Scanning

本文の内容について、最も適切な答えや語句を (A) ～ (C) から選びなさい。

1. Which of these is NOT mentioned as a benefit of coffee?

(A) It helps people lose weight.

(B) It helps us remember things better.

(C) It prevents heart disease.

2. All of these are true about Kaldi EXCEPT _____.

(A) he came from Ethiopia

(B) he made drink from a certain tree's berries

(C) he was a goat farmer

3. New hybrid coffee beans are being used because they are _____ than regular beans.
(A) cheaper (B) harder to grow (C) stronger and more resistant to disease

3 Conversation

A Listen and Write

30

次の会話を聞いて、(　　) に単語を書きなさい。

W: I'm tired. I could really use a cuppa joe.
M: Me too. Let's go to the coffee shop across the [1](　　　　　　).
W: Sounds good. Let me [2](　　　　　　) my jacket. Oh, no!
M: What's [3](　　　　　　)?
W: I forgot my [4](　　　　　　)!
M: No worries. It's on me.

B Listen and Choose

31

質問を聞いて、(　　) に単語を書き、最も適切な応答を (A) ～ (C) から選びなさい。

1. (　　　　　) (　　　　　) the man and woman going (　　　　　　) (　　　　　　)?
(A) Get some coffee (B) Look for the woman's jacket (C) Take a nap

2. (　　　　　) (　　　　　) (　　　　　　) to pay for the man and woman's (　　　　　　)?
(A) The man will pay for both.
(B) The woman will pay for both.
(C) They will pay for their own coffee(s).

Notes **a cuppa joe (= a cup of coffee)**「1杯のコーヒー」 **no worries**「心配しないで」 **it's on me**「おごるよ」 **take a nap**「うたた寝をする」

4 Text Completion

次の文章を読んで、空所に入れる最も適切なものを (A) ～ (C) から選びなさい。

There are many ways to make coffee at home. The most popular way is to use a "drip" coffee machine. Hot water is poured __1__ top of ground coffee beans. The liquid then drips into a carafe. Another way is to use a "Moka Pot." Water is heated in the pot __2__ it boils and produces steam. The steam then moves through the beans, making a cup of coffee. Some people use what is called a "French press." Coffee beans soak in hot water for a few minutes. Then a plunger is pushed __3__ the beans, leaving a cup of coffee.

1. (A) in (B) on (C) under
2. (A) after (B) to (C) until
3. (A) down on (B) inside and (C) over but

Notes **carafe**「カラフ」ドリップしたコーヒーを受けるガラス容器 **Moka Pot**「モカポット」コーヒー沸かし器 **French press**「フレンチプレス」湯を注ぐコーヒー抽出器 **plunger**「プランジャー」コーヒーポットの押し出し部分

5 Grammar

A イラストに合うように、(　　)内の最も適切な前置詞を選び、英文を完成しなさい。

1. There is a window (above / on / up) the desk.
2. There is a desk (behind / beside / over) the bed.
3. (Against / Down / Under) the desk, a cat is sleeping.
4. There are two pictures on the wall (at / beside / on) the door.
5. A laptop is (at / in / on) the desk.
6. There are some textbooks (beside / from / next) the laptop.
7. There are some clothes (by / on / over) the bed.
8. There is a coffee table (among / between / through) the TV and the sofa.
9. An alarm clock is (at / on / to) the bedside table.
10. An air conditioner has been installed (at / by / over) the ceiling.

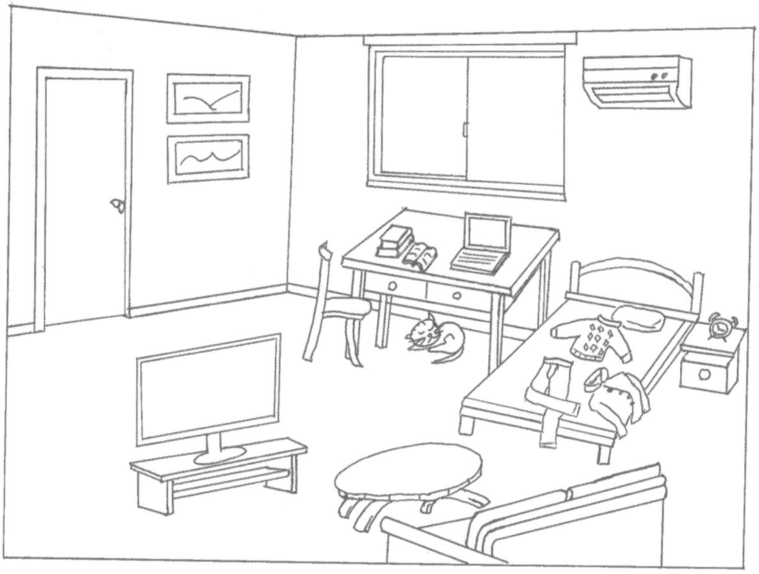

B 空所に入れる時を表す前置詞を語群から選び、英文を完成しなさい。

at	in	on	×（前置詞不要）

1. Jennifer was born (　　　) 2001.
2. Justin has to go to the dentist (　　　) Friday morning.
3. Hurry up! The movie starts (　　　) seven.
4. We had a meeting (　　　) last Monday.
5. I worked (　　　) four hours this morning.
6. I'll be back (　　　) a minute.
7. What will you do (　　　) next weekend?
8. Her birthday is (　　　) August 12th.

C in, at, on のいずれかの前置詞に続く語句を下から選び、空所に入れて英文を完成しなさい。

~~the afternoon~~	the airport	the cover of the book	the pool	the sky	the 40th floor

e.g. My uncle usually takes a nap in the afternoon.

1. My office is in this high-rise building. It is ____________________.
2. Monica is reading a novel. The author's name is ____________________.
3. There are some children swimming ____________________.
4. My flight arrives at 10:20 a.m. Could you pick me up ____________________?
5. Today is a sunny day. There isn't a cloud ____________________.

D 前半に続く後半を (a) 〜 (d) から選び、英文を完成しなさい。

1. We went camping in _____.
2. Colin looked for his keys _____.
3. Sally will meet you at the store _____.
4. Coffee helps provide a boost _____.

(a) in the box under the desk
(b) next to the library
(c) of energy during the day
(d) the forest near the lake

6 Writing

A 日本語に合うように、(　　) 内の語句を並べ替えなさい。

1. Americans (coffee / cups / day / drink / every single / of / three), making the U.S. the leading coffee consumer in the world.
アメリカ人は毎日3杯のコーヒーを飲み、アメリカを世界の主要なコーヒー消費国にしています。

2. A large number (countries / developing / farmers / in / make / of / their living) growing coffee beans.
発展途上国の多くの農業従事者は、コーヒー豆を育て生計を立てています。

B 次の質問に、(　　) 内の語句を使って答えなさい。

1. Which do you prefer tea or coffee? Why?
(like to drink / enjoy the taste / every morning)

2. When you go shopping, do you check where the food comes from? Why or why not?
(worry about / from different countries / check on the label)

Grammar Spotlight

▶前置詞

名詞・代名詞の前に置き、時・場所・理由・方法などを表します。

1. 時

We work **from** 9 a.m. **to** 5 p.m.
Jeff will be back **in** an hour.
Michael will be there **at** 9 o'clock.
Sarah will hold a birthday party **on** the 11th of June.
You should be back **by** eight.
I've been living here **for** twenty years.

☞ tomorrow, yesterday, next, last には前置詞を使いません。

× I graduated from college **on last** Saturday.
○ I graduated from college **last** Saturday.

2. 場所

The clock is hanging **on** the wall.
We spent a quiet evening **at** home.
The shopping center is **near** the station.
There is a sea **between** England and France.
Sophie lives **in** the house **by** the river.

3. 理由

I am pleased **at** your success.
Parker is in bed **with** a cold.

4. 方法・手段

Grace goes to school **by** bike or **on** foot.
Please write **with** a black ballpoint pen.

Unit 11
Which Came First, Lighters or Matches?

▶ conjunctions

火を人工的に起こす手法は、人類史上最大の発明かもしれません。その後、いつでもどこでも簡単に、瞬時に着火できる便利な道具が発明されました。それはライターとマッチですが、どちらが先に発明されたのでしょうか。

Warm-up

次の質問に英語で答えなさい。

1. Which do most people use these days, lighters or matches?
2. What do you think is the most important invention in history?

1 Vocabulary

英文の（　　）に入れる最も適切な単語を語群より選び、(A) ～ (J) で答えなさい。

(A) dangerous	(B) exploded	(C) flammable	(D) forbidden	(E) friction
(F) humanity	(G) modern	(H) passengers	(I) pistol	(J) wooden

1. The storage bin was filled with (　　) materials, which mysteriously caught fire.
2. (　　) computers are much smaller and faster than computers were in the 1990s.
3. When you rub two sticks together, you create (　　), which causes heat that you can use to start a fire.
4. The (　　) bridge was made from trees cut down over 200 years ago.
5. Kenji's job is interesting but (　　). He takes photos of rhinos, Komodo dragons, and other wild animals.
6. A terrorist bomb (　　) near my condominium, killing ten people.
7. Several (　　) were injured when the express train came to a sudden stop.
8. I want to find a job where I can work for the good of (　　).
9. Please put out that cigarette. In this ward, smoking while walking on the street is (　　).
10. In America, you can easily buy a (　　) at almost any gun shop.

2 Reading 32

Some people believe that fire is humanity's greatest invention. They may be right. Thanks to fire, we can heat our homes, cook foods, drive our cars, and even fly to the moon. People have always looked for better ways to make fire quickly. Two inventions that people still use today are the match and the lighter. Today's question is: Which came first, the lighter or the match?

Lighters were invented almost four hundred years ago, in the 17th century. They didn't look at all like modern lighters. They were made from the parts of old pistols. In 1823, a German chemist, Johann Wolfgang Döbereiner, created the first real lighter, which he called "Döbereiner's lamp."

The first friction match, the successor of which we use today, was invented three years later by English inventor John Walker. Before the friction match, people put flammable chemicals on wooden sticks. When these chemicals were combined, the sticks would catch fire. But these burning sticks were not only difficult to make; they also smelled very bad and were dangerous to use.

Over the years, inventors have come up with safer and more dependable matches and lighters. Both are still widely used today, and will probably be used for many years to come.

Notes **Johann Wolfgang Döbereiner**「ヨハン・ヴォルフガング・デーベライナー」ドイツの化学者 **friction match**「摩擦マッチ」 **come up with**「考案する」 **for many years to come**「これらから先何年もの間」

Reading Comprehension

A True or False

次の英文が本文の内容と一致する場合は T、一致しない場合は F を選びなさい。

1. Most people believe that fire isn't really an important invention. [**T F**]

2. Matches were invented many years before lighters were created. [**T F**]

3. The first matches were a little dangerous and difficult to make. [**T F**]

B Skimming and Scanning

本文の内容について、質問に対する最も適切な答えを (A) ～ (C) から選びなさい。

1. When were lighters made from pistol parts created?
(A) In the 17th century (B) In the 18th century (C) In the 19th century

2. When were friction matches invented?
(A) In 1820 (B) In 1823 (C) In 1826

3. How did the first matches catch fire?
(A) By combining chemicals
(B) By rubbing sticks together
(C) By using a lighters

3 Conversation

A Listen and Write

33

次の会話を聞いて、(　　) に単語を書きなさい。

M: Do you have any liquids?

W: Just this bottle of water that I [1](　　　　　) at a kiosk here in the airport.

M: That's fine, then. Do you have anything flammable with you?

W: I don't think so. Oh, wait. There might be a lighter in the [2](　　　　　) of my purse.

M: Let's take a [3](　　　　　). There it is. I'll have to take that.

W: I'm really sorry. I forgot all about it. I gave up [4](　　　　　) over a year ago.

B Listen and Choose

34

質問を聞いて、(　　) に単語を書き、最も適切な応答を (A) ～ (C) から選びなさい。

1. (　　　　　) (　　　　　) the man (　　　　　) the woman (　　　　　)?

(A) Do you have any liquids?

(B) Do you have anything flammable with you?

(C) Is there a lighter in your purse?

2. (　　　　　) (　　　　　) the woman (　　　　　)?

(A) Because she forgot her lighter on the airplane.

(B) Because she forgot to take the lighter out of her purse.

(C) Because she lost her lighter.

Notes **flammable**「可燃性の」 **there it is**「あった」

4 Text Completion

次の文章を読んで、空所に入れる最も適切なものを (A) ～ (C) から選びなさい。

Not too long ago, you could bring almost anything on an airplane with you. __1__, however, many items are forbidden when you travel by air. For example, you cannot carry any sharp objects like scissors. __2__, you cannot take flammable items that might catch fire or explode. This includes lighters and matches. You are also not allowed to bring more than 100 milliliters of a liquid. But if you bought a bottle of water or soda at the airport, __3__.

1. (A) Although (B) Nowadays (C) Therefore

2. (A) Moreover (B) Subsequently (C) Though

3. (A) it's quite a bit more expensive

(B) you can bring it with you onto the airplane

(C) you have to open your bags for inspection

Notes **not too long ago**「つい最近まで」 **by air**「飛行機で」 **inspection**「検査」

5 Grammar

A (　　) 内の適切な接続詞を選び、英文を完成しなさい。

1. It is a sunny day, (but / or) the wind is cold.
2. (Although / Because) Norah waited for Jack, he did not come.
3. (Before / Once) you learn how to ride a bicycle, you will never forget how to do it.
4. Which would you like for breakfast, cereal (and / or) toast?
5. Laura just moved to a new city, (and / because) everything is still exciting to her.
6. Mark didn't see the famous castle, (for / nor) did he see the old cathedral.
7. Kitty went to the farmers' market (for / so) she could buy some fresh vegetables.

B (　　) 内の最も適切な接続詞を選び、英文を完成しなさい。

1. Sally plays not only the guitar (and / but / or) also the violin.
2. Edward will (both / either / neither) drive to the office or take a bus today.
3. I don't know whether Maria will come (and / but / or) not.
4. We have time to see a movie (and / but / nor) visit the museum.
5. My father neither drinks (and / or / nor) smokes.

C 次の 2 文を、and / but / or のいずれかでつないで 1 文にしなさい。

1. Nancy usually goes to school by bicycle. She took the bus this morning.

   ....

2. The black deluxe car stopped. The movie star got out.

   ....

3. Would you like to go out for dinner? Shall I make something?

   ....

4. Billy wants to go for a hike. He has to work today.

   ....

5. Hurry up. You will be late for the game.

   ....

D 空所に入れる最も適切な接続副詞を語群より選び、英文を完成しなさい。

As a result	However	Moreover	On the other hand	Otherwise

1. We'd better leave now. ____________________, we will be late for the concert.
2. Sally studied hard for the exam. ____________________, she got a very high score.
3. Ben hurt his leg early in the game. ____________________, he still managed to score two goals!
4. On one hand, living in the country is very relaxing. ____________________, it can be a little inconvenient.
5. Knowing a foreign language allows you to communicate with local people. ____________________, it can introduce you to a new culture.

E 前半に続く後半を (a) ～ (d) から選び、英文を完成しなさい。

1. Jack did not finish his assignment on time and _____.
2. The home team finally won the game even though _____.
3. You can finish the activity in class; alternatively, _____.
4. The lighter was actually invented _____.

(a) before the match was
(b) subsequently, he had to talk with the teacher
(c) they had been losing at the half
(d) you can do it for homework

6 Writing

A 日本語に合うように、(　　) 内の語句を並べ替えなさい。

1. The first lighter was invented in 1823, marking (an era / could be / created / fire / of / the start / when) in an instant.
最初のライターが 1823 年に発明され、すぐに火がつけられる時代の始まりになりました。

2. John Walker's first friction match didn't get (and expensive / attention / because of / mix / much / of / the dangerous) ingredients.
ジョン・ウォーカーの最初の摩擦マッチは、危険で高価な材料を混ぜたものなので、あまり注目されませんでした。

B 次の質問に、(　　) 内の語句を使って答えなさい。

1. What are some common uses for lighters or matches?
(people often use / to make a fire / they are camping)

2. Should governments sell cigarettes and alcohol to the country's citizens? Why or why not?
(bad for the health / it seems strange to me / promote healthy living)

Grammar Spotlight

▶接続詞

等位接続詞と従属接続詞があり、語と語、句と句、文と文をつなぎます。

1. 等位接続詞：語・句・文を対等に結びます。(and, but, for, nor, or)

Sandra likes shopping **and** traveling.
Tracy wanted to study abroad, **but** she wasn't able to.

2. 従属接続詞：文（従属節）を文（主節）につなぐ働きをします。

名詞節を導く if, that, whether と、副詞節を導く although, as, because, if, since, until, when, while などがあります。

I don't know **if** Beth will come on time.　　＜名詞節＞
If it rains tomorrow, we will postpone the event.　　＜副詞節＞

3. 間違いやすい表現

「〜の間」

Lucas had a good time **during** summer vacation.　　（前置詞で、後ろは名詞）
Jim waited **while** Mia was shopping.　　（接続詞で、後ろは S+V）

「〜のために」

The event was called off **because of** heavy rain.　　（前置詞）
Lisa was late for class **because** the bus was delayed.　　（接続詞）

Unit 12
Why Is Meat from Pigs Called "Pork"?

▶tag questions / modifiers

言葉のルーツを調べると、歴史や文化などの背景を知ることがあります。英語では豚肉をポーク、牛肉をビーフと言い、動物とその肉では全く異なる呼び方をします。これは不思議ですね。英語の言葉の成り立ちについて考えてみましょう。

Warm-up

次の質問に英語で答えなさい。

1. Do you like to eat meat? If so, what kind? If not, why not?
2. How often do you eat out at restaurants?

1 Vocabulary

英文の（　　）に入れる最も適切な単語を語群より選び、(A) ～ (J) で答えなさい。

(A) evolved	(B) combination	(C) indigenous	(D) livestock	(E) options
(F) provide	(G) raise	(H) responsible	(I) vegetarian	(J) wealthy

1. Thousands of (　　) languages spoken by native peoples around the globe are rapidly disappearing.
2. After my husband retired, he started to (　　) chickens in our backyard and sell the eggs to our neighbors.
3. How the poor, homeless man became a (　　) landowner is a fascinating story.
4. "Bicycle" is a (　　) of two old Greek and Latin words: bi, which means "two," and cycle, which means "circle."
5. The producer on a movie is (　　) for hiring the director, actors, and camera crew, and for handling the money.
6. Some people still cannot accept the idea that human beings and apes (　　) or developed from the same common ancestor.
7. Cows, horses, and other (　　) were moved to higher ground to avoid the flooding.
8. My 10-year-old daughter suddenly announced that she was becoming a (　　) and would no longer eat any meat.
9. Today, in most coffee shops, customers have dozens of coffee (　　) to choose from.
10. During the pandemic lockdowns and online classes, schools had to (　　) laptops to children who didn't have their own.

2 Reading

35

English learners are often surprised (and puzzled) to find out that English has different words for animals and for the meat that comes from them. Students must learn that the meat of pigs is called pork, the meat of cows is called beef, the meat of chickens is sometimes known as poultry, and the meat of sheep is called mutton.

The reason for this is that many languages are used to make English. Today, English is a combination of French, German, ancient Latin and Greek, and an indigenous language called Anglo-Saxon. Hundreds of years ago, when English was first developing as a language, people from different social "classes" used words from different languages to talk about the same thing. Poor people, who were responsible for raising livestock, used words of German origin—cow, pig, and sheep—for the names of animals.

But the wealthy landowners who ate the food from these animals thought that some languages, such as French and Latin, were better than others. They used "superior" French and Latin words for the names of the different kinds of meat, which they called *porc*, *boeuf*, and *mouton*. These "foreign" words eventually evolved into the English words pork, beef, and mutton.

Over the centuries, people continued to use these two "classes" of words. Nowadays, the more "common" words like cow and pig are still used to talk about the animals while the more "fancy" words like beef and pork stand for the meat the animals provide.

Notes **poultry**「ポウルトリー」鶏肉 **a combination of**「～の組み合わせ」 **class**「階層」 **be responsible for**「～に責任がある」 **wealthy landowner**「裕福な地主」 **stand for**「～を表す」

Reading Comprehension

A True or False

次の英文が本文の内容と一致する場合は T、一致しない場合は F を選びなさい。

1. In English, there are different words for animals and for the animals' meat. [**T F**]

2. English is mostly made up of only two languages, French and Greek. [**T F**]

3. Rich people preferred Anglo-Saxon words to words from other languages like French, Latin, or Greek. [**T F**]

B Skimming and Scanning

本文の内容について、空所に入れる最も適切な語句を (A) ～ (C) から選びなさい。

1. The meat of sheep is known as _____.

(A) beef (B) mutton (C) poultry

2. A long time ago, landowners often used _____ words to talk about their food.

(A) German (B) Greek (C) French and Latin

3. The word we use today to talk about the meat of cows comes from the French word _____.

(A) boeuf (B) porc (C) mouton

3 Conversation

A Listen and Write 36

次の会話を聞いて、(　　) に単語を書きなさい。

W: What would you like for dinner?
M: Actually, I'm [1](　　　　　　　　) of making tacos.
W: Oh really? What [2](　　　　　　　　) of tacos are you making?
M: Nothing fancy. Maybe [3](　　　　　　　　) or chicken?
W: Actually ... I'm a vegetarian.
M: That's right. Sorry. I forgot. Don't [4](　　　　　　　　). We'll have eggplant pasta instead.

B Listen and Choose 37

質問を聞いて、(　　) に単語を書き、最も適切な応答を (A) ～ (C) から選びなさい。

1. What are they (　　　　　　　　) (　　　　　　　　)?
(A) What they will eat for dinner
(B) Where they will go for dinner
(C) Whom they will invite for dinner

2. (　　　　　　) (　　　　　　) the man (　　　　　　) "We'll have eggplant pasta instead"?
(A) Because the woman doesn't eat meat.
(B) Because the woman is not hungry.
(C) Because the woman only eats pasta.

Notes **tacos**「タコス」メキシコ料理 **nothing fancy**「特別なものは何もない」 **vegetarian**「菜食主義者」 **eggplant pasta**「ナスのパスタ」

4 Text Completion

次の文章を読んで、空所に入れる最も適切なものを (A) ～ (C) から選びなさい。

More and more people these days are choosing not to eat meat, __1__? Vegetarianism is becoming increasingly popular. That's why many shops and restaurants now provide no-meat food options. For example, there is a kind of ham made from tofu. There is also a hamburger made of beans! Being a vegetarian is becoming __2__ concerned about religion and more and more about health. Most vegetarians think that eating only vegetables __3__.

1. (A) are they　(B) aren't they　(C) don't they
2. (A) bigger and bigger　(B) less and less　(C) more and more
3. (A) is healthier than eating meat
(B) is cheaper than buying beef or pork
(C) is not as healthy as an all-meat diet

Notes **these days**「最近」 **vegetarianism**「菜食主義」 **increasingly**「ますます」 **all-meat diet**「すべて肉の食事」

5 Grammar

A (　　) 内の適切な付加疑問を選び、英文を完成しなさい。

1. It's warm today, (is it / isn't it)?
2. You don't have any questions, (do you / don't you)?
3. You can speak English really well, (can you / can't you)?
4. She is from Canada, (is she / isn't she)?
5. You didn't attend class yesterday, (are you / did you)?

B 文の終わりに適切な付加疑問を付けて英文を完成しなさい。

e.g. That was delicious, wasn't it?

1. You didn't come to school yesterday, ________________?
2. This activity isn't so difficult, ________________?
3. Peggy is always shopping for new clothes, ________________?
4. Mike reads a lot of comic books, ________________?
5. Paul and Emily have been to America, ________________?

C (　　) 内の最も適切な修飾句を選び、英文を完成しなさい。

1. As people read more books, they become (easier and easier / smarter and smarter).
2. His English pronunciation is improving. It is getting (better and better / more and more).
3. I've been busy recently. I have (less and less / more and more) time to hang out with my friends.
4. (Fewer and fewer / Less and less) people go to the movies these days.
5. It is a close game. The fans are becoming (bigger and bigger / more and more) excited.

D 語群より形容詞を選び、「比較級 + and + 比較級」の形にして英文を完成しなさい。

cold	hard	heavy	hot	old

e.g. I am eating too much! I am getting fatter and fatter.

1. A: Wow! What is the temperature?
B: I'm not sure, but it's getting ____________________________ and muggier and muggier.
2. A: How is the job search going?
B: It seems to be getting ____________________________ to find a job.
3. It's December now, so the weather will be growing ____________________________.
4. Many wines improve with age as they get ____________________________.
5. Her bags got ____________________________ as she went from store to store in the mall.

E 前半に続く後半を (a) ～ (d) から選び、英文を完成しなさい。

1. It is becoming more and more _____.
2. My doctor told me that I should start _____.
3. Japanese is adopting _____.
4. Summer is almost here! Every day it is _____.

(a) eating less and less meat
(b) popular to grow vegetables at home
(c) getting warmer and warmer
(d) more and more foreign words

6 Writing

A 日本語に合うように、(　　) 内の語句を並べ替えなさい。

1. In English, animals have (about / different / names / talking / the meat / we're / when) they provide. "Pigs" becomes "pork" and "cows" becomes "beef."
英語において動物は、それらが与える肉について私たちが話すときには、異なる名前を持ちます。「豚」は「ポーク」、「牛」は「ビーフ」になります。

2. French's influence on English goes back to the Norman Conquest of Britain in 1066. That is (became / French words / many / of / part / the English / when) language.
英語に対するフランス語の影響は、1066 年のイギリスのノルマン・コンクエストにさかのぼります。その時、多くのフランス語の単語が英語の一部になりました。

B 次の質問に、(　　) 内の語句を使って答えなさい。

1. What do you do to stay healthy?
(I usually / Lately, I have been)

2. These days, more and more people are choosing to be a vegetarian. What do you think about that?
(becoming a vegetarian is / chemicals in meat processed food / difficult to find healthy meat products)

Grammar Spotlight

▶付加疑問文

1. be 動詞の場合

肯定文＋[, be 動詞の否定形]＋[主語を示す代名詞] ?

It's a lovely day, **isn't it**?

The film was fantastic, **wasn't it**?

否定文＋[, be 動詞の肯定形]＋[主語を示す代名詞] ?

She isn't cleaning her room, **is she**?

These parfaits aren't too sweet, **are they**?

2. 一般動詞の場合

肯定文＋[, don't / doesn't / didn't]＋[主語を示す代名詞] ?

Owen plays soccer, **doesn't he**?

She had a great time, **didn't she**?

否定文＋[, do / does / did]＋[主語を示す代名詞] ?

He doesn't like tomatoes, **does he**?

Cathy didn't make today's dinner, **did she**?

3. 命令文の場合

[, will you?]を付ける

Open the door, **will you**?

4. Let's の場合

[, shall we?]を付ける

Let's play soccer, **shall we**?

▶修飾句

比較級 and 比較級

「ますます（だんだん）～」 と、程度が次第に増えることを表します。

It is getting **warmer and warmer** day by day.

Betty has become **busier and busier** these days.

The wind was getting **stronger and stronger**.

less and less ～

「ますます～でなくなる」と、程度が徐々に減っていくことを表します。

I miss her **less and less** as every day goes by.

比較級 and 比較級が名詞を修飾することもあります。

Fewer and fewer people are traveling abroad these days.

More and more children are playing games.

Unit 13
Can You Wang a "Welly"?

▶ relative pronouns / relative adverbs

雨の日でも、おしゃれなレインブーツで足元を飾ると、気持ちが明るくなります。ブーツを英国人はウェリー (welly) と言います。スポーツとしてブーツを投げる競技もあります。ブーツの由来について考えてみましょう。

Warm-up

次の質問に英語で答えなさい。

1. Do you play any sports? What sport do you want to try?
2. What unusual sports do you have in your country?

1 Vocabulary

英文の（　）に入れる最も適切な単語を語群より選び、(A) ～ (J) で答えなさい。

(A) aristocrats	(B) current	(C) dialect	(D) goal	(E) indicate
(F) introduced	(G) originally	(H) outdoor	(I) taste	(J) technique

1. Did you know that Pepsi Cola was (　　) called "Brad's Drink"?
2. When I was young, our family spent the summer vacation doing (　　) activities like camping and hiking.
3. McDonald's was (　　) to Japan in 1971. I was one of its very first customers.
4. Jane Austen's novels often deal with (　　), that is, wealthy landowners often related to royalty.
5. As an American, I have a hard time understanding some people from Northern England when they speak in their (　　).
6. Tatsuya's (　　) is to get a Ph.D. in medical research.
7. Your excellent test scores (　　) that you can go to any university you want.
8. Do you know who is the (　　) men's world figure-skating champion?
9. Today's *Science Daily* says that scientists have developed a new (　　) to make fresh drinking water from seawater.
10. Margot's (　　) in music is different from mine. I like country, but she prefers jazz.

2 Reading 38

Dark clouds in the sky indicate it is about to rain. That means it's time to get out our umbrellas and raincoats. On days when it really pours, many of us put on rubber rain boots, too. These boots were once mostly black, but today they come in all colors and designs to fit every purpose and taste.

Rain boots were introduced to England by the Duke of Wellington in the early 19th century. Wellington was a national war hero. He was an army general who defeated Napoleon at Waterloo, one of the most famous military battles in history. Originally, these boots were hand-crafted from leather. They were mostly worn by rich aristocrats for horseback riding and other outdoor activities. Eventually, the boots were made of rubber and worn by people of all classes. The boots today are known as wellies (one boot is a "welly"), named after the Duke of Wellington.

In the 1970s, people in the West Country of England came up with an unusual new sport, which they called "Welly Wanging." The goal is to throw ("wang" in the local dialect) a "welly" as far as you can. Welly Wanging has become more and more popular over the years. Today, people from all over the world participate. There is even an annual World Welly Wanging Championship. It is held in a place called Upperthong Village, where the sport originated. The current record for tossing a welly is 63.98 meters for men and 40.87 meters for women. Both records were set in 1996.

Notes **the Duke of Wellington**「ウェリントン公爵」 **army general**「陸軍元帥」 **Warterloo**「ワーテルロー」 **hand-crafted**「手作りの」 **welly**「ウェリントンブーツ」 **Welly Wanging**「ウェリー・ワンギング」ブーツを投げてその距離を競う **as far as one can**「できるだけ遠くに」 **World Welly Wanging Championship**「ブーツ投げ世界選手権」

Reading Comprehension

A True or False

次の英文が本文の内容と一致する場合は T、一致しない場合は F を選びなさい。

1. Wellies were named after a British general and war hero. [T F]
2. Welly Wanging became a sport in 1996. [T F]
3. Welly Wanging is only played by English people. [T F]

B Skimming and Scanning

本文の内容について、空所に入れる最も適切な語句を (A) ～ (C) から選びなさい。

1. The original wellies were made by hand from _____.
   (A) cloth (B) leather (C) rubber
2. The sport of Welly Wanging started in the _____ Country of England in a place called Upperthong Village.
   (A) East (B) North (C) West
3. The World Welly Wanging Championship takes place _____.
   (A) every ten years (B) once a year (C) twice a year

3 Conversation

A Listen and Write 39

次の会話を聞いて、(　　) に単語を書きなさい。

W: It looks as if it's going to rain. Look at those dark [1] (　　　　　　).
M: You should take an umbrella with you, just in case.
W: Good idea. And a raincoat, too. By the way, [2] (　　　　　　) are my rain boots?
M: They are in the bedroom closet, aren't they?
W: No. I [3] (　　　　　　), but they aren't there.
M: Oh, that's right. I [4] (　　　　　　) them in the garage to dry them out.

B Listen and Choose 40

質問を聞いて、(　　) に単語を書き、最も適切な応答を (A) ～ (C) から選びなさい。

1. Why does the woman think (　　　　) (　　　　) (　　　　) in the afternoon?
(A) The rain has started to fall.
(B) The sky has clouded over.
(C) The sky is clearing up.

2. Why did the man (　　　　) (　　　　) (　　　　) in the (　　　　)?
(A) He forgot to.
(B) The closet was full.
(C) They were wet.

Notes　**just in case**「念のため」　**by the way**「ところで」

4 Text Completion

次の文章を読んで、空所に入れる最も適切なものを (A) ～ (C) から選びなさい。

How to Throw a Welly

There are several different ways to "wang" a "welly." The first—known as the "one-handed technique"—is the most popular. As its name tells you, you toss the welly with one hand. Next comes the "two-handed technique," __1__ is good for heavy boots. The third way to wang a welly is called the "between-the-legs technique." People __2__ are new to this unusual sport seem to prefer this method. Finally, there is the "backward throw technique," __3__ you toss the boot with both hands backwards over your head.

1. (A) what　(B) which　(C) who
2. (A) when　(B) which　(C) who
3. (A) that　(B) where　(C) which

Notes　**betweeen-the-legs technique**「脚の間から投げるテクニック」　**toss ... backwards**「～を後ろに投げる」　**over one's head**「頭越しに」

5 Grammar

A (　　) 内の適切な関係代名詞を選び、英文を完成しなさい。

1. She is the exchange student (which / who) comes from France.
2. I received the letter (that / whom) you sent me.
3. What did you do with the money (that / whom) your father gave you?
4. That is the woman (who / whom) was on TV last night!
5. I have met a movie star (whose / that) name I can't remember.
6. The man (which / who) stole my money had a tattoo on his arm.
7. That's (what / which) I'm talking about.
8. She helped the woman (who / whose) lives next door.

B (　　) に入れる適切な関係副詞 (when / where / how / why) を選び、英文を完成しなさい。

1. That's the apartment (　　　　　　　) I used to live.
2. Andy will never forget the day (　　　　　　　) he met Cathy.
3. Do you know the reason (　　　　　　　) Leo was so pleased last night?
4. Would you please tell me (　　　　　　　) you made this delicious curry?
5. The hotel (　　　　　　　) I will stay in Los Angeles is new.

C who / which / where のどれかを使って、２つの文を１つにしなさい。

e.g. I have a friend. She can play the violin. → I have a friend who can play the violin.

1. The waiter served us. He was very polite.

....

2. Michael grew up in a small village. He went back there recently.

....

3. The new hall will be opened on May 1. It can hold 3,000 people.

....

D 前半に続く後半を (a) 〜 (d) から選び、英文を完成しなさい。

1. I went to the store where _____.
2. She is the woman who _____.
3. I didn't understand the question that _____.
4. I didn't enjoy the movie that _____.

(a) the teacher asked
(b) traveled to the U.S. last year
(c) we saw last weekend
(d) you bought your computer

6 Writing

A 日本語に合うように、(　　) 内の語句を並べ替えなさい。

1. The boot (as / gets / from / its / name / known / the “welly”) the Duke of Wellington, who was a war hero in the early 1800s.

「ウェリー」として知られているブーツはウェリントン公爵から名付けられていますが、彼は1800年代初頭、戦争の英雄でした。

2. “Welly Wanging” is a (are / competitors / in which / required / sport / throw / to) a Wellington boot as far as they can.

「ウェリー・ワンギング」は、競技者がウェリントンブーツをできるだけ遠く投げることを求められるスポーツです。

B 次の質問に、(　　) 内の語句を使って答えなさい。

1. Would you like to try Welly Wanging? Why or why not?

(I am interested in [I am curious about] / how far / toss a rubber boot)

2. What interesting sport have you heard about that you would like to try?

(want to try / I saw it being played / it is a sport)

Grammar Spotlight

▶関係詞

1. 関係代名詞

関係代名詞は「接続詞と代名詞」の働きをする語で、「名詞を説明する節」と「説明される名詞（先行詞）」を結びつけます。

Helen is **the sales assistant who** works in a shoe store. ＜主格＞
I have **a friend whose** father is a famous shoemaker. ＜所有格＞
I saw **the shoes that** Paul bought yesterday. ＜目的格＞

先行詞	主格	所有格	目的格
人	who / that	whose	whom / who / that
物	which / that	whose	which / that

2. 関係副詞

関係副詞は「接続詞と副詞」の働きをする語で、「前置詞＋関係代名詞」で言い換えられます。

I will never forget **the day when** I met Karen. (= on which) ＜時＞
That is **the place where** we got married. (= in which) ＜場所＞
I don't know **the reason why** she is crying. (= for which) ＜理由＞
Let me show you **how** I designed these rain boots.
(= the way [in which]) ＜方法＞

・この場合、in which は省略されます。

Unit 14
Why Do We Shake Hands?

▶participles / participle constructions

握手はビジネスやスポーツなど様々な場面で行われます。欧米では、笑顔で、相手の目を見ながら、右手で握手をします。握手は相手と良い関係を築く不思議な力があります。握手をする習慣が、どのように始まったのかを考えてみましょう。

Warm-up

次の質問に英語で答えなさい。

1. Do you shake hands when you meet someone?
2. What other ways do people from different countries greet each other?

1 Vocabulary

英文の（　　）に入れる最も適切な単語を語群より選び、(A) ～ (J) で答えなさい。

(A) admiration	(B) affection	(C) customary	(D) empty	(E) extend
(F) fascinating	(G) grasp	(H) involved	(I) polite	(J) significance

1. In Japan, and now in many other places, it is (　　) to take off your shoes when you enter a house.
2. When you shake hands, it is best to (　　) the other person's hand firmly, but not too firmly.
3. I have great (　　) and respect for the nurses and doctors who have worked so hard during this crisis.
4. What is the (　　) of the new company policy? What does it mean for employees?
5. Children need lots of love and (　　) to grow up happy and healthy.
6. We were really impressed by how (　　) and efficient our server was. She went out of her way to make our dinner a pleasant one.
7. The verb (　　) can mean to stretch out a hand to reach something, to make something last longer, or to offer something to someone.
8. How (　　)! What an interesting story today's speaker had to tell!
9. All the people (　　) in the demonstration are very concerned about keeping endangered wild animal species from dying out.
10. It is very weird to watch a baseball game on TV and see that the stands are almost completely (　　).

2 Reading 41

In most Western countries—and in many other parts of the world as well—it is customary for people to shake hands when they meet and greet each other. Shaking hands is also done to "seal a deal"—that is, to reach an agreement. As you know, to shake hands, the two people involved extend their right hand. Then they grasp each other's hands and do a gentle up-and-down motion a few times. So how did this custom get started?

Shaking hands has a long, fascinating history. There are drawings and paintings of people shaking hands from as long ago as the fifth century A.D. The tradition started back in the days when people used to fight with swords. Usually, people kept their sword in a scabbard. This was a long, hollow cover that hung from a belt on their left side. This made it easy for "fighters" to pull the sword out with their right hand. But what if the two people had no intention of fighting or using their swords to hurt each other? In that case, they held out their empty right hands and shook them in the same way that we do today.

Over the centuries, shaking hands has developed greater significance. It's a polite gesture of affection, admiration, and trust. But some newer forms of greeting have also emerged recently. Today, it's common to see people doing "high-fives" or "fist bumps" when they meet or congratulate each other. During the COVID era, we also practiced "elbow bumps," which were supposed to keep us safe.

Notes **seal a deal**「契約を結ぶ」 **extend = hold out**「差し出す」 **a few times**「数回」 **place in a scabbard**「さやに納める」 **what if ...?**「もし～だったどうしますか」 **in that case**「その場合は」 **high-five**「ハイタッチ」 **fist bump**「フィストバンプ」拳と拳を合わせる挨拶 **elbow bump**「エルボーバンプ」ひじタッチ

Reading Comprehension

A True or False

次の英文が本文の内容と一致する場合は T、一致しない場合は F を選びなさい。

1. Shaking hands as a greeting is only done in America and Europe. [**T F**]
2. Shaking hands can be used when you agree on something with someone. [**T F**]
3. Shaking hands can be used as a sign of respect. [**T F**]

B Skimming and Scanning

本文の内容について、最も適切な語句や答えを (A) ～ (C) から選びなさい。

1. When you shake hands, it is customary to hold each other's hands and _____.
   (A) move your hands gently up and down
   (B) move your hands in a large circle
   (C) move your hands quickly side to side
2. What was the original purpose of shaking hands?
   (A) To show the other person that you are not an enemy
   (B) To show the other person that you have a sword
   (C) To show the other person that you want to talk about something

3. Which of these is NOT mentioned as a newer form of greeting?
(A) Elbow bumps (B) Fist bumps (C) Finger crossing

3 Conversation

A Listen and Write

42

次の会話を聞いて、(　　) に単語を書きなさい。

W: Nice to [1](　　　　　) you, I'm Ellie.
M: Hi, Ellie. My name is Taro. [*shaking hands*]
W: Where are you from?
M: Well, I was born in Japan, but I lived in the U.S. for several years when I was in [2](　　　　　) school.
W: Oh, so, [3](　　　　　) a returnee. That's why you can speak English so well.
M: Partly, yes. But mostly it's because I have [4](　　　　　) a lot of time studying.

B Listen and Choose

43

質問を聞いて、(　　) に単語を書き、最も適切な応答を (A) ～ (C) から選びなさい。

1. (　　　　　) (　　　　　) the man (　　　　　) (　　　　　)?
   (A) Canada (B) Japan (C) The U.S.
2. Why does the woman (　　　　　) the man (　　　　　) (　　　　　) English well?
   (A) Because he spent time in the U.S.
   (B) Because he studies so hard.
   (C) Because he was born abroad.

Notes **returnee**「帰国子女」 **that's why**「だから～だ」

4 Text Completion

次の文章を読んで、空所に入れる最も適切なものを (A) ～ (C) から選びなさい。

Handshakes are the most common greeting. But most countries have their own unique ways to greet others. Believe it or not, in Tibet, __ 1 __ out your tongue when you greet someone is polite! This shows that you are not one of the country's evil, black-tongued ancient rulers. In the Philippines, young people put an older person's hand against their forehead in a greeting __ 2 __ the *Mano*. At any rate, __ 3 __ is a wonderful way to show your respect for the culture of any country that you visit.

1. (A) stick (B) sticking (C) stuck
2. (A) call (B) called (C) calling
3. (A) shaking hands with everyone you meet (B) sticking out your tongue
   (C) using the proper form of greeting

Notes **believe it or not**「信じられないかもしれないが」 **ruler**「支配者」 **at any rate**「とにかく」

5 Grammar

A (　　) 内の適切な分詞を選び、英文を完成しなさい。

1. After listening to his speech, Amanda felt (inspired / inspiring).

2. My two-hour bus ride to work every day is very (tired / tiring).

3. Sam couldn't believe how terrible the food at the stall was. The ramen was (disgusted / disgusting).

4. I am so (bored / boring). There is nothing to do here!

5. Ellie was (pleased / pleasing) to get your message.

6. The (shocked / shocking) news was reported in all the media.

7. We were (shocked / shocking) to hear that the president was retiring to become a painter.

8. Kevin was awakened by a (rung / ringing) bell.

B 2つの英文を、分詞 (-ing / -ed) を用いて1つの英文にしなさい。

1. She is cleaning the room. She is singing a song.
→ She is cleaning the room (　　　　　　　　) a song.

2. The church was built in the 1700s. It now needs renovation.
→ (　　　　　　　　) in the 1700s, the church now needs renovation.

3. I was walking in the park. I saw a lot of squirrels.
→ (　　　　　　　　) in the park, I saw a lot of squirrels.

4. The novel is written in simple English. It is easy to read it.
→ (　　　　　　　　) in simple English, the novel is easy to read.

C 分詞構文（-ing 句）を用いて、英文を完成しなさい。

e.g. After I finished my homework, I played games.
→ Finishing my homework, I played games.

1. When I arrived at the supermarket, I found it was closed.
→ ______________________________, I found it was closed.

2. As he felt tired after his long walk, he went to bed early.
→ ______________________________, he went to bed early.

3. While I was walking down the street. I met Maria by chance.
→ ______________________________, I met Maria by chance.

4. She bought an electric bike. She cycled home.
→ ______________________________, she cycled home.

D 語群から動詞を選び、適切な分詞にして、英文を完成しなさい。

call	inspire	make	tire	wear

1. Her life story was so (　　　　　　　　) that the director decided to make a movie about her.

2. After three hours on the train, Sally felt quite (　　　　　　　　).

3. Catherine works in a bakery (　　　　　　　　) fancy cakes for birthdays and other celebrations.

4. Paul Cézanne is an artist often (   ) "the Father of Modern Art".

5. A woman (   ) a blue dress opened the door.

E 前半に続く後半を (a) ～ (d) から選び、英文を完成しなさい。

1. Smoking rooms cannot be _____.

2. A firm handshake shows that you are _____.

3. The children were excited to hear that they would be _____.

4. The teacher caught the students _____.

(a) going to Europe for vacation

(b) found in this building

(c) passing notes in class

(d) pleased to meet the other person

6 Writing

A 日本語に合うように、(　　) 内の語句を並べ替えなさい。

1. Shaking hands used to be a sign of friendship and trust (going to / his sword / person / take / that / the other / wasn't) out to fight.
握手はかつて、相手の人は戦うために剣を抜くつもりがない、という友情と信頼の証でした。

2. Before sports games and matches, you will (each / hands / other / players / see / shaking / with), which is considered proper sporting behavior.
スポーツのゲームや試合の前に、選手たちがお互いに握手をしているのを見るでしょうが、それは適切なスポーツの振る舞いと考えられています。

B 次の質問に、(　　) 内の語句を使って答えなさい。

1. When was the first time you shook hands with someone? How did it make you feel?
(practiced shaking hands / was uncomfortable for me)

2. Some people think that Japanese people these days are greeting each other less than they once did. Do you agree? Why or why not?
(used to greet / not greet people as much / a little shocked)

Grammar Spotlight

▶分詞

分詞は名詞を修飾する働きと、補語になる働きがあります。

1. 名詞を修飾

現在分詞（-ing）:「～している」

The mother got up to soothe her **crying** **baby**.

I know **the woman** **walking** over there.

過去分詞（-ed）「～された」

Nick has **a camera** **made** in Japan.

2. 補語として主語の動作・状態を説明

The movie is **interesting**.

Karen was **bored**.

The news was **shocking** to her.

He looked **satisfied** with the results of the experiment.

▶分詞構文

分詞構文では、現在分詞または過去分詞が、接続詞と動詞を兼ねた働きをします。

1. 時、原因・理由、付帯状況、条件、譲歩があります。

時「～している間に、～時に」

Waiting at the bus stop, I met Oliver.

= **While I was waiting** at the bus stop, I met Oliver.

原因・理由「～なので」

Having nothing left to do, Sarah went home.

= **Since Sarah had** nothing left to do, she went home.

付帯状況「～しながら」

Ryan sat on the sofa, **watching** television.

= Ryan sat on the sofa, **and he watched** television.

条件「～なら」

Turning to the left, you will find the bakery.

= **If you turn** to the left, you will find the bakery.

譲歩「～だけれども」

Wearing a coat, I feel cold.

= **Though I am wearing** a coat, I feel cold.

2. 否定の分詞構文

Not knowing what to say, I remained silent.

= **As I didn't know** what to say, I remained silent.

3. 受動態の分詞構文

Written in simple English, the article is easy to understand.

= **As the article is written** in simple English, it is easy to understand.

Unit 15
What Did the First Webcam See?

▶discourses / subjunctives

ウェブカメラは、リアルタイムでのテレワークやリモート会議をはじめ、動画のライブ配信、友人とのチャットなど、さまざまなシーンで利用されているアイテムです。最初のウェブカメラは、何を映すために発明されたのかを考えてみましょう。

Warm-up

次の質問に英語で答えなさい。

1. Do you use your phone or computer to communicate with your friends?
2. How much time do you spend each week on social networking applications?

1 Vocabulary

英文の（　　）に入れる最も適切な単語を語群より選び、(A) ～ (J) で答えなさい。

(A) awake	(B) cost	(C) frames	(D) hallway	(E) letter
(F) located	(G) postmark	(H) purpose	(I) resolution	(J) stamps

1. This new camera model has a higher (　　), which means there is much greater detail in the pictures.
2. Henry's real (　　) for taking French class was to spend time with his girlfriend, not to learn French.
3. I didn't get much sleep last night. I was (　　) all night watching YouTube videos.
4. When we were in elementary school, our teachers would make us stand out in the (　　) if we were too noisy in class.
5. With smartphone GPS, you can find where it is (　　).
6. I am working part-time and saving up for a new computer. I want the best and fastest computer, but that will (　　) a lot of money.
7. In the old days, if you wanted to send a message to someone, you had to write and send a "snail-mail" (　　).
8. Some people like to collect foreign coins; others like to collect foreign (　　). They find it interesting to see the many different styles used in different countries.
9. When you receive a package, you can always check the (　　) to see where the package came from.
10. A movie actually shows 24 different pictures every second—that's 24 fps, or (　　) per second. This is what creates the illusion that what is on the screen actually moving.

2 Reading 44

These days we often use web cameras to talk with our friends, family, and coworkers online. We can do this because today's web cameras are small, cheap, and capable of performing many wonderful functions. Some web cameras take pictures in 4K, which means that the picture resolution is approximately 4,000 pixels wide (3840×2160). They can also record full-color pictures at 60fps—that is, 60 frames per second. Some cameras can even track a person who is talking so that users can walk and talk at the same time.

The purpose of the first web camera was quite different, however. In 1991, University of Cambridge researchers Quentin Stafford-Fraser and Paul Jardetzky would often work late at night. To stay awake, they drank cup after cup of coffee. The coffee area was located in the hallway outside their office. When they went out to get a cup, they were often disappointed to find that the pot was empty. This gave the two researchers a bright idea. Why not create a way to constantly monitor how much coffee was left in the pot?

So they used their imaginations and came up with a camera that, when set next to the coffee pot, could transmit black-and-white pictures to their desktop PCs. This was the original web camera. The old saying "Necessity is the mother of invention" was surely right in this case. This webcam could take just one very low-resolution picture per second. Nevertheless, it was an important advance in computer and communication technology.

Notes **picture resolution**「画像解像度」 **pixels wide**「画素幅」 **60 frames per second**「1秒間に60フレーム」 **at the same time**「同時に」 **stay awake**「目を覚ましている」 **bright idea**「名案」 **why not ...?**「〜したらどうですか」 **come up with**「考案する」 **old saying**「古いことわざ」 **in this case**「この場合には」 **low resolution**「低解像度」

Reading Comprehension

A True or False

次の英文が本文の内容と一致する場合はT、一致しない場合はFを選びなさい。

1. Web cameras have become an essential part of our lives. [**T** **F**]
2. The first-ever web camera was designed so that people could communicate with one another. [**T** **F**]
3. The first web camera was more advanced than today's web cameras. [**T** **F**]

B Skimming and Scanning

本文の内容について、空所に入れる最も適切な語句を (A) 〜 (C) から選びなさい。

1. The term "4K" means that the resolution of the pictures the camera takes is about _____.
   (A) 4,000 pixels in total (B) 4,000 pixels tall (C) 4,000 pixels wide
2. Quentin Stafford-Fraser and Paul Jardetzky worked _____.
   (A) at a university (B) for a computer maker (C) in company office

3. The first web camera was used _____.
  (A) to find out who was drinking all the coffee
  (B) to see if there was any coffee remaining in a coffee pot
  (C) to show workers how to make coffee in a coffee pot

3 Conversation

A Listen and Write 45

次の会話を聞いて、(　　)に単語を書きなさい。

W: Excuse me. How much is this web cam?
M: That's last year's model. It's on sale at $ [1](　　　　　).
W: I see. How about this one right [2](　　　　　)?
M: That's the latest model. It sells for $ [3](　　　　　).
W: Wow! Why is it so pricey?
M: It has motion tracking and can [4](　　　　　) pictures in 4K.

B Listen and Choose 46

質問を聞いて、(　　)に単語を書き、最も適切な応答を (A) ～ (C) から選びなさい。

1. What is the woman (　　　　　) (　　　　　)?
  (A) A car　　(B) A web camera　　(C) An internet service

2. What does the woman mean (　　　　　) (　　　　　) (　　　　　) "pricey"?
  (A) Cool　　(B) Expensive　　(C) Large

Notes　**latest model**「最新モデル」　**motion tracking**「モーショントラッキング」動作追跡

4 Text Completion

次の文章を読んで、空所に入れる最も適切なものを (A) ～ (C) から選びなさい。

In the old days, if you wanted to talk with a friend or family member who lived far away, you ___1___ them a letter. People used to especially look forward to ___2___ mail from someone living in a different country. They liked to see the different stamps and postmarks from each place. Because communication technology is so advanced, talking to someone on the other side of the world is now ___3___, even though this means some older pleasures are disappearing.

1. (A) are used to　　(B) will need to　　(C) would write
2. (A) receive　　(B) receiving　　(C) received
3. (A) easy, quick, and free
  (B) even more expensive and difficult
  (C) no longer necessary

Notes　**postmark**「(郵便の) 消印」　**no longer**「もはや～ない」

5 Grammar

A (　　)に単語を入れて、直接話法を間接話法の英文にしなさい。

1. She said, "I'm leaving in five minutes."
→ She said (　　　　) (　　　　) leaving in five minutes.

2. Ms. Simmons said, "Can you come to the office this afternoon?"
→ Ms. Simmons asked if (　　　　) (　　　　) come to the office this afternoon.

3. Mary said to Frank, "What do you want for dinner?"
→ Mary asked Frank what (　　　　) (　　　　) for dinner.

4. Henry said to his children, "Be quiet!"
→ Henry told his children (　　　　) (　　　　) quiet.

5. The doctor said, "You must maintain a healthy diet."
→ The doctor said that (　　　　) (　　　　) to maintain a healthy diet.

B (　　)に単語を入れて、間接話法を直接話法の英文にしなさい。

1. Sally said she wanted to go home.
→ Sally said, "(　　　　) (　　　　) to go home!"

2. My teacher asked if we had any questions.
→ My teacher said, "(　　　　) (　　　　) (　　　　) any questions?"

3. His mother asked him where he had gone.
→ His mother said to him, "Where (　　　　) (　　　　) (　　　　)?"

4. He told me to hurry up or I would be late for school.
→ He said to me, "(　　　　) (　　　　) or (　　　　) (　　　　) be late for school!"

5. She asked us if we were from Canada.
→ She said to us, "(　　　　) (　　　　) from Canada?"

C (　　)内の適切な語句を選び、仮定法の英文を完成しなさい。

1. If I (am / were) you, I would stop drinking so much soda.
2. If Kate (is / were) truly my friend, she wouldn't talk behind my back.
3. She talks as if she (know / knew) everything.
4. I wish I (practice / had practiced) the violin harder when I was younger.
5. I suggested that Catherine (sings / sing) the new song at tonight's party.
6. If Brian (were to go / had not gone) to the store, we would have nothing for dinner.

D 同じ意味を表すように、(　)に単語を書いて英文を完成しなさい。

1. { If he had not advised me, I could not have done the work.
(　　　　) his (　　　　), I could not have done the work.

2. { He didn't study very hard, so he didn't pass the exams.
If he (　　　　) (　　　　) harder, he would (　　　　) (　　　　) the exams.

3. { If it should rain tomorrow, I will stay at home.
(　　　　)(　　　　) rain tomorrow, I will stay at here.

4. I'm sorry I didn't have any humor in my presentation.
   I (   ) I (   ) had some humor in my presentation.

5. If she were a wise person, she would not say such a thing at the meeting.
   A (   ) (   ) (   ) not say such a thing at the meeting.

E 前半に続く後半を (a) ～ (d) から選び、英文を完成しなさい。

1. Judging from the look of the sky, _____.
2. I would've bought the carpet at a bargain _____.
3. If you should have any questions, _____.
4. My boss treats me _____.

(a) as if I were his family
(b) it is going to rain soon
(c) price if there hadn't been such a line
(d) please don't hesitate to contact our office

6 Writing

A 日本語に合うように、(　　) 内の語句を並べ替えなさい。

1. In 1991, the webcam was invented at the University of Cambridge to (know / let / not / or / researchers / the coffee pot / whether) in the hallway was full.
   1991 年に、廊下のコーヒーポットが一杯かどうかを研究者たちに知らせるために、ケンブリッジ大学でウェブカメラが発明されました。

2. The world's first webcam transmitted a live (computers / connected to / of / picture / the coffee pot / the network / to).
   世界で最初のウェブカメラは、ネットワークにつながっているコンピュータにコーヒーポットのライブ画像を送信しました。

B 次の質問に、(　　) 内の語句を使って答えなさい。

1. Do you think you spend too much time using social media? Why or why not?
   (spend a lot of time / stayed up late / surfing YouTube)

2. These days, more and more people send New Year's cards by email instead of regular mail. What do you think about that?
   (prefer digital New Year's cards / easier to send)

Grammar Spotlight

▶話法

直接話法：話者の発言をそのまま伝えます。

間接話法：人が言ったことを自分の言葉に言い換えて伝えます。

1. 時制の一致

間接話法で主節の動詞が過去形のとき

He said, "I **am** going to use a web camera."
He said (that) he **was** going to use a web camera.

2. 人称代名詞の変化

She said to me, "**I** like **your** new design."
She told me (that) **she** liked **my** new design.

3. 命令文、疑問文の話法の書き換え

She said to me, "Please **copy** the document."
She **told** me **to copy** the document.

She said to me, "**Are you** tired?"
She **asked** me **if [whether] I was** tired.

He said to me, "Who **called me**?"
He **asked** me who **had called him**.

▶仮定法

仮定法は、現実にありえないことを「もし～なら、…だろう」「もし～だったら、…だっただろう」という意味で、仮定の状況を述べる表現です。

1. 仮定法現在：現在・未来についての仮定

I **suggested** that he (should) **leave** at once.
It is **necessary** that she (should) **go** there.

・要求・提案を表す動詞 ask, demand, request, suggest, require, insist や、必要・重要を表す形容詞 necessary, important などに続く that 節では、動詞を原形にします。

2. 仮定法過去：現在の事実に反することの仮定

If I had computer skills, I **could get** a better job.

・If ＋ S ＋過去形, S ＋ could [would, might, should] ＋動詞の原形

3. 仮定法過去完了：過去の事実に反することの仮定

If I had had more time, I **could have talked** to him.

・If ＋ S ＋ had ＋過去分詞, S ＋ could [would, might, should] ＋ have ＋過去分詞

4. 仮定法の慣用的表現

Without your advice, I **couldn't finish** the report.
If it had not been for the traffic jam, they **could have arrived** on time.
Lena behaves **as if** he **were** the boss.

Answers to Everyday Questions 3 <Intermediate>

身近な不思議を英語で学ぶ　＜中級＞ [B-941]

1　刷　2023年1月15日

著　者　アーノルド・アラオ　Arnold Arao
三原　京　Kei Mihara
巳波　義典　Yoshinori Miwa
木村　博是　Hiroshi Kimura

発行者　南雲一範　Kazunori Nagumo
発行所　株式会社　南雲堂
〒162-0801　東京都新宿区山吹町361
NAN'UN-DO Co., Ltd.
361 Yamabuki-cho, Shinjuku-ku, Tokyo 162-0801, Japan
振替口座：00160-0-46863
TEL: 03-3268-2311（営業部:学校関係）
03-3268-2384（営業部:書店関係）
03-3268-2387（編集部）
FAX: 03-3269-2486

編集者　加藤　敦

装　丁　Nスタジオ

組　版　Office haru

検　印　省　略

コード　ISBN978-4-523-17941-2　C0082

Printed in Japan

E-mail nanundo@post.email.ne.jp
URL https://www.nanun-do.co.jp/